朗文
外研社
练 习 册

新概念英

NEW CONCEPT ENGLISH
W O R K B O O K

New Edition 新版

Developing Skills
培养技能

3

亚历山大（L. G. ALEXANDER）（英）
金斯伯里（ROY KINGSBURY）（英）　何其莘　合作编著

外语教学与研究出版社

LONGMAN 朗文

京权图字：01－2007－0733

图书在版编目(CIP)数据

新概念英语练习册 3／(英)亚历山大(Alexander, L.G.)等合作编著 . — 北京：外语教学与研究出版社，2002.1 (2007.1 重印)
ISBN 978－7－5600－2482－0

Ⅰ. 新… Ⅱ. 亚… Ⅲ. 英语—习题 Ⅳ. H319.6

中国版本图书馆 CIP 数据核字 (2007) 第 006233 号

universal tool·unique value·useful source·unanimous choice

悠游外语网
www.2u4u.com.cn

外研社全新推出读者增值服务网站，独家打造双语互动资源

欢迎你：
○ 随时检测个人的外语水平和专项能力
○ 在线阅读外语读物、学习外语网络课程
○ 在线观看双语视频、名家课堂、外语系列讲座
○ 下载外语经典图书、有声读物、学习软件、翻译软件
○ 参与社区互动小组，参加线上各种比赛和联谊活动
○ 咨询在线专家，解决外语学习中的疑难问题

此外，你还可以通过积累购书积分、兑换图书、电子书、培训课程和其他增值服务……

你有你"优"，你的优势就是你的拥有。即刻登录，抢先体验！

出 版 人：于春迟
出版发行：外语教学与研究出版社
社　　址：北京市西三环北路 19 号 (100089)
网　　址：http://www.fltrp.com
印　　刷：北京市鑫霸印务有限公司
开　　本：787×1092　1/16
印　　张：9.25
版　　次：2001 年 12 月第 1 版　2009 年 12 月第 14 次印刷
印　　数：460001—480000 册
书　　号：ISBN 978－7－5600－2482－0
定　　价：9.90 元
＊　　　＊　　　＊

朗文　　新概念英语（新版）
外研社

NEW CONCEPT ENGLISH (New Edition)
WORKBOOK 3 练习册 3

双语版出版人：吴天祝
合作出版人：李朋义
合作编著者：亚历山大 (L.G. Alexander)，金斯伯里 (Roy Kingsbury)，何其莘 (He Qixin)
责任编辑：蔡女良（朗文）　任小玫（外研社）
封面设计：梁若基

外语教学与研究出版社
培生教育出版北亚洲有限公司　　联合出版

Lesson 5   The facts

A   Special difficulties

Each sentence below is incomplete. Choose the one word or phrase (a, b, c or d) which best completes the sentence, and write it in. 圈出正确答案,并填在横线上。

1 Not only _____ the telephone number, but he had also forgotten his mobile phone.

   (*a*) he forgot   (*b*) did he forget   (*c*) he had forgotten   (*d*) had he forgotten

2 Never _____ such a lot of rubbish!

   (*a*) I have read   (*b*) do I read   (*c*) have I read   (*d*) I read

3 Seldom _____ a man like James, a man who will do anything for anyone.

   (*a*) you meet   (*b*) you have met   (*c*) you might meet   (*d*) will you meet

4 I only _____ when I got home that I should have posted these letters this morning.

   (*a*) remember   (*b*) remembered   (*c*) did remember   (*d*) have remembered

5 Hardly _____ her lecture when she picked up her notes and left the room.

   (*a*) she finished   (*b*) had she finished   (*c*) did she finish   (*d*) she has finished

6 Only after listening to him for an hour _____ what a great musician he was.

   (*a*) we realized   (*b*) we have realized   (*c*) did we realize   (*d*) would we realize

7 Rarely _____ the chance to see these animals close up again in the future.

   (*a*) did you get   (*b*) you get   (*c*) you've got   (*d*) will you get

8 We not only _____ all the sandwiches but we ate all their cake too.

   (*a*) finished   (*b*) have finished   (*c*) would finish   (*d*) had finished

B   Comprehension

Read each short text, the questions and the four possible answers. Choose the best answer to each question, a, b, c *or* d. 圈出正确答案。

Text 1 (A newspaper announcement)

The editor admits reluctantly that in publishing yesterday's article about the escaped puma, the newspaper failed to provide the facts its regular readers normally expect. Not only did the article mislead readers, but it has also become clear that some of the facts were incorrect.

1 What is the editor doing?

   (*a*) Reprinting yesterday's article.

   (*b*) Asking for readers' comments.

   (*c*) Giving his readers more facts.

   (*d*) Apologizing to his readers.

2 How much of the article was incorrect?

   (*a*) All of it.

   (*b*) Most of the facts.

   (*c*) A lot of it.

   (*d*) Some of the facts.

Text 2 (A radio announcement)

News has just come in that an intruder broke into the presidential palace early this morning in an attempt to assassinate the president. The facts surrounding the incident are so far unclear, but we have learned that a man was arrested. He has not yet been identified.

1 What did the man do?
- (a) He assassinated the president.
- (b) He entered the palace illegally.
- (c) He tried to interview the president.
- (d) He and friends surrounded the palace.

2 What happened to the man?
- (a) He was identified.
- (b) He was injured.
- (c) He was killed.
- (d) He was caught.

Text 3 (An introduction)

I would like to welcome our speaker today, Karl Day, as a very successful journalist, and now, with his first novel ready to go to press, a successful novelist, we hope. Karl assures me that he has gone to extremes to obtain the exact information he needed for this, his first novel.

1 Why is Karl already well known?
- (a) Because he writes novels.
- (b) Because he speaks at meetings.
- (c) Because he writes for the press.
- (d) Because he is always welcome.

2 What is he just about to publish?
- (a) A journal.
- (b) His first work of fiction.
- (c) Some exact research.
- (d) An article about novel writing.

C   Key structures: *a, an, the* and *some*

Read each sentence carefully. In each one, identify the one underlined word or phrase (A, B, C or D) that must be changed for the sentence to be correct. 圈出句子中错误的词或词组。

1 <u>Yangtze River</u>, which rises in <u>the Kunlun Mountains</u>, is <u>the</u> longest river in <u>China</u>.
      A   B   C   D

2 According to <u>an</u> information I read about <u>the</u> city, it was <u>founded</u> in <u>the</u> 1st century AD.
              A   B   C   D

3 She was <u>so</u> keen to hear <u>latest news</u> that when she heard <u>it</u> she almost missed <u>the</u> facts.
         A   B   C   D

4 <u>The journalist</u> I spoke to was writing <u>an article</u> with <u>the title</u> '<u>Best way</u> to become a journalist'.
      A   B   C   D

5 I have <u>any</u> good <u>advice</u> for <u>people</u> who want to give up <u>smoking</u>.
      A   B   C   D

6 <u>The holiday industry</u> in <u>Australia</u> has increased <u>a</u> great deal in <u>some</u> past twenty years.
          A   B   C   D

Lesson 7　　Mutilated ladies

A　Vocabulary and Special difficulties

Each sentence has an underlined word or phrase from Lesson 7. Choose one of the words or phrases (a, b, c, d) which best keeps the meaning of the original sentence if it is substituted for the underlined word or phrase. Put a ring round a, b, c *or* d. 以下句子选自第 7 课的课文。圈出与划线的词或词组最相近的答案。

1　She has so many accidents because she is so <u>careless</u>.

　　(*a*)　worried　　(*b*)　cautious　　　(*c*)　negligent　　(*d*)　lazy

2　For many years my uncle ran a very <u>successful</u> engineering business.

　　(*a*)　rewarding　　(*b*)　expensive　　(*c*)　persuasive　　(*d*)　profitable

3　Imagine my <u>dismay</u> when I got home to find that my apartment had been broken into.

　　(*a*)　sadness　　(*b*)　anger　　　　(*c*)　pleasure　　　(*d*)　impatience

4　After the accident, my back <u>was very painful</u> for a long time.

　　(*a*)　was a pain　　(*b*)　hurt a lot　　(*c*)　was injured　　(*d*)　wounded me

5　A <u>spokeswoman</u> for the company promised that they would investigate our complaint.

　　(*a*)　speaker　　(*b*)　lecturer　　　(*c*)　actress　　　(*d*)　representative

6　Why is it that small children are so <u>energetic</u>?

　　(*a*)　effective　　(*b*)　vigorous　　　(*c*)　active　　　(*d*)　busy

7　If you think that you can never replace that priceless painting, don't <u>despair</u>. All is not lost!

　　(*a*)　cry　　　　(*b*)　make a noise　　(*c*)　lose hope　　(*d*)　be desperate

8　All the students in our sports teams are very <u>athletic</u>.

　　(*a*)　fit　　　　(*b*)　strong　　　　(*c*)　fast　　　　(*d*)　physical

9　<u>Fortunately</u>, when my car broke down in the country, I had my mobile with me.

　　(*a*)　Accidentally　(*b*)　Fatally　　　(*c*)　Luckily　　　(*d*)　By chance

10　This report <u>concerns</u> a man who lives in London, but works in Paris.

　　(*a*)　worries　　(*b*)　is anxious about　(*c*)　has an effect on　(*d*)　is about

B　Key structures: the simple past

Each sentence below is incomplete. Beneath each sentence you will see four words or phrases (a, b, c, d). Choose the one word or phrase that best completes the sentences. Put a ring round a, b, c *or* d *and write in the word or phrase.* 圈出正确答案, 并填在横线上。

1　When the police arrived, they _____ the scene of the crime very carefully.

　　(*a*)　have examined　(*b*)　were examining　(*c*)　were examined　(*d*)　examined

14

2 'Last year,' said the spokesman, 'we _____ out £5 million in insurance claims.'

    (*a*) pay   (*b*) have paid   (*c*) paid   (*d*) were paying

3 The wallet that I found _____ £100 in five-pound notes.

    (*a*) was contained   (*b*) has contained   (*c*) contained   (*d*) containing

4 The fire brigade came quickly and a fireman _____ the girl's dog from the river.

    (*a*) just rescued   (*b*) has just rescued   (*c*) was just rescuing   (*d*) was just rescued

5 My mother _____ the cake out of the oven when she dropped it.

    (*a*) took   (*b*) was taking   (*c*) had taken   (*d*) was taken

6 When I _____ home yesterday evening I was so tired I went straight to bed.

    (*a*) got   (*b*) was getting   (*c*) had got   (*d*) have got

C Comprehension

Read each of these conversations. After each conversation there is a question with four possible answers. Decide which one is the best answer to the question. 选出正确答案。

1 Tim: I was taking the dog for a walk, and I stopped to get some money from a cash machine. I put in my credit card and it chewed it up!

    Susan: So it just ate it, didn't it?

    What happened to Tim's credit card?

    (*a*) His dog ate it.

    (*b*) The machine destroyed it.

    (*c*) He just lost it somewhere.

    (*d*) Someone stole it.

2 Woman: Where does Mary's fiancé Alfred come from?

    Man: Well, originally he came from Newcastle, but he's lived in London for a very long time.

    Where was Alfred born?

    (*a*) A long way from Mary's fiancé.

    (*b*) In the same place as Mary.

    (*c*) Newcastle.

    (*d*) London.

3 Betty: Why do you do all your cooking in a microwave?

    Ann: My father used to run a small business selling microwave ovens and my mother always cooked with a microwave, so I learned to, too.

    What did Ann's father do?

    (*a*) He was a chef.

    (*b*) He taught his daughter to cook.

    (*c*) He used to run a lot.

    (*d*) He sold microwave ovens.

Lesson 9   Flying cats

A   Comprehension

Read this text, think of the word which best fits each space and write it in. Use only one word in each space. 用正确的词填空，每空仅填一个词。

DON'T GIVE ME ANY ADVICE

The way people lead 1 _____ lives nowadays never fails 2 _____ surprise me. While people in the past used to solve their own problems, nowadays there is 3 _____ shortage of advice about anything you care to think of. 4 _____ a result, people almost seem to have stopped thinking for 5 _____.

I suffer a little 6 _____ forgetfulness, I'm afraid, and 7 _____ certain people notice it, they want to ignore my independence and offer 8 _____ advice. 'I'll tell you 9 _____ you can improve your memory,' they say, and they start their advice. I am generally a patient sort 10 _____ person, so I just stand or sit there listening like some kid being lectured to by an adult.

You know, I am always a little suspicious 11 _____ people who are so eager to give advice. I wonder first of all what they want, and then wonder 12 _____ they are as eager to accept advice themselves.

Advice which is given without 13 _____ asked for is called 'unsolicited advice' in English, and the less you ask friends for advice, the more 14 _____ you are to get it. As far as I know, no one has ever died 15 _____ taking too much advice, although acting on the wrong advice has probably hurt quite a number of people. It would be absolutely fascinating to find out 16 _____ much damage unsolicited advice has done in our modern world!

There are certain people, of course, 17 _____ advice we should always listen to. A friend of mine decided to take 18 _____ parachuting and went on a course. The instructor, who was a paratrooper, an army parachutist, immediately earned everyone's respect and they all quickly learned to do 19 _____ he told them, 20 _____ silly or unreasonable it sounded. The reason was simple: they knew that his advice might save their lives.

18

B Special difficulties: *so*, *such*, *such a* and *such an*

Complete the second sentence (in each pair), using the word given, so that it has a similar meaning to the first sentence. You must use the word in bold. We have done the first for you. 用所给的黑体词完成以下句子, 使每组中的两句话表达相似的意思。

1 Squirrels are so rare here that we don't often see one.
   sight
   Squirrels *are such a rare sight* here that we don't often see one.

2 The weather was so horrible that we came home early.
   such
   We had _____ that we came home early.

3 My aunt's cat is such an affectionate animal that everyone loves him.
   so
   My aunt's cat _____ that everyone loves him.

4 John is so independent that he never listens to advice.
   person
   John _____ that he never listens to advice.

5 The men had such difficulty crossing the river that they had to turn back.
   difficult
   The men found _____ the river that they had to turn back.

6 Her jewellery is so fantastic that everyone admires it.
   wears
   She _____ that everyone admires it.

C A letter

Situation: When a friend said she was going away for a week, you rashly offered to look after her cat. Now you find that you can't do it. *Write the friend a letter of about 80 words explaining why you can't look after the cat after all. Do not bother to write your address or the date.* 情景: 当一个朋友说她要出门一周时, 你草率地提出要为她看管她的猫。 现在你发现无法做到这一点。写一封 80 个词左右的信, 说明你为什么无法看管她的猫, 不必写地址和日期。

_____

_____

_____

_____

_____

_____

_____

Lesson 11　Not guilty

A　Vocabulary

Each sentence below is incomplete. Choose the one word or phrase (a, b, c *or* d) *which best completes the sentence.* 选词填空。

1 The customs officer asked me, 'Have you anything to _____, madam?'

   (*a*) give   (*b*) declare   (*c*) explain   (*d*) state

2 The top on this bottle is far too tight. I can't _____ it.

   (*a*) untie   (*b*) unwrap   (*c*) unfasten   (*d*) unscrew

3 Why is it that so many 'important' people who work for the government are so _____?

   (*a*) official   (*b*) office   (*c*) officious   (*d*) offer

4 A good teacher learns to be _____ even when his pupils make the same mistakes.

   (*a*) tolerate   (*b*) tolerable   (*c*) tolerating   (*d*) tolerant

5 'Jane, your room's in a _____ mess! Clear it up right now!'

   (*a*) dreadful   (*b*) dread   (*c*) dreaded   (*d*) dreading

6 In the 18th century _____ used to sail over from France and hide contraband tobacco and wine and rum in caves in the south of England.

   (*a*) thieves   (*b*) muggers   (*c*) robbers   (*d*) smugglers

B　Adverbs and adjectives

Read each sentence carefully. In each one, identify the one underlined word or phrase (A, B, C *or* D) *that must be changed for the sentence to be correct.* 圈出句子中错误的词或词组。

1 From everything <u>that</u> the officer said <u>to me</u>, he <u>clear</u> thought I was <u>mad</u>.
              A   B   C   D

2 Bob felt <u>extremely</u> <u>confidently</u> because he was <u>sure</u> he had done <u>well</u> in the job interview.
          A   B   C   D

3 When the lady teacher <u>angrily</u> accused John <u>of</u> <u>cheating</u>, he looked at her <u>guilty</u> and admitted it.
                A   B C   D

4 'Come <u>on</u>, John! Be <u>brave</u>! You know you can <u>do</u> it,' he shouted <u>encouraging</u> at his son.
        A   B   C   D

5 I can <u>honest</u> say that I only <u>narrowly</u> missed <u>hitting</u> the car coming <u>fast</u> in the other direction.
         A   B   C   D

6 Speaking <u>sarcastic</u> to <u>young</u> children doesn't work; they <u>simply</u> don't understand <u>sarcasm</u>.
         A   B   C   D

C Key structures: indirect speech

Complete the second sentence (in each pair), using the word given, so that it has a similar meaning to the first sentence. You must use the word in bold. We have done the first for you. 用所给的黑体词完成以下句子, 使每组中的两句话表达相似的意思。

1 'The man is obviously a hardened criminal,' Karl said to me.

clearly

Karl said that *the man was clearly* a hardened criminal.

2 'I don't mind helping you,' he said to me.

told

He _____ mind helping me.

3 'Do you want the porter to carry your baggage?' the receptionist asked us.

our

The receptionist asked _____ baggage.

4 'How many bottles of perfume are there in your case?' the Customs officer asked the man.

much

The customs officer asked _____ in his case.

5 'Where have you been?' Jim's mother wanted to know.

asked

Jim's mother _____ been.

D Composition

Read the text on page 54 of the Students' Book again. Imagine you are the Customs officer who stopped the writer and went through his case. Write a brief account (100-140 words) of what happened from your point of view. Begin like this: 'I was on duty recently when a young man came through the Green Channel and I thought he looked like …' 重读课文。以故事中海关官员的身份重述课文 (100 至 140 个词), 用指定的句子开头。

_____

_____

_____

_____

_____

_____

_____

_____

_____

_____

Lesson 15   Fifty pence worth of trouble

A   Comprehension

*Read this article about a fire fighter. Choose from the list **A-G** (in the box below) the sentence which best summarises each part (**1-5**) of the article. There is an example at the beginning, and there is one extra sentence which you do not need to use.* 阅读以下关于消防队员的故事，然后从方框中选择可以用来归纳总结故事各段的词组和句子。方框中的一项选择是多余的。

A day in the life of a fire fighter
Dan Jones talks about his job

Example | G

I wasn't very good at school. I couldn't do maths and I couldn't write very well. But I was good at sports. With my pocket money I saved up and bought a racing bicycle and I kept very fit.

1 | |

I first applied to join the fire brigade when I was 16. I was too young, but they advised me to try again two years later. So I worked on a building site for two years and then I was accepted into the fire brigade.

2 | |

At first I couldn't get used to climbing long ladders or putting on breathing equipment, but I finally managed to do everything. I remember the first time I put on breathing equipment, I put it on the wrong way. The others laughed, but I quickly learned the right way!

3 | |

We regularly fight fires, of course, and it can be dangerous sometimes. But I've done all the correct training, and I would rather do this than anything else I can think of. The important thing to remember always is that fire is dangerous and can kill: it can kill fire fighters as well as anyone else.

4 | |

Apart from fighting fires, we also do other things. Last week, for example, we were able to save the lives of three children by cutting them out of a wrecked car. And then there was a young boy firmly stuck with his arm down a drain cover in the High Street. Apparently he had rolled up his sleeve and put his hand down to try and get a fifty pence piece which had bounced down. We rubbed some special grease on his arm and managed to free him quite easily.

5 | |

I really like the job and I know that people appreciate what we fire fighters do. The only thing is that we aren't really paid enough. I'm saving up to get married and buy an apartment, but it's going to take a long time.

A	Not only fire fighting
B	First experiences
C	A major train accident
D	Fire fighters don't earn much
E	I couldn't wait to apply
F	Fighting fires
G	<u>No good at school</u>

B   Key structures: *could, was able to* and *managed to*

Complete the second sentence (in each pair), using the word given, so that it has a similar meaning to the first sentence. You must use the word in bold. We have done the first for you. 用所给的黑体词完成以下句子，使每组中的两句话表达相似的意思。

1   After three days the climbers succeeded in reaching the summit of the mountain.
   managed
   After three days the climbers *managed to reach the summit* of the mountain.

2 I was a very good swimmer when I was younger.

could

I _____ when I was younger.

3 The shops could only stay open because the owners paid protection money.

able

The shops _____ because the owners paid protection money.

4 We have never succeeded in beating our nearest school at football.

managed

We _____ at football.

5 If they had enough money, they could employ someone to paint their house.

painted

If they had enough money, they _____.

6 John wanted to buy himself a bicycle, but he couldn't save up enough.

able

John _____ to buy himself a bicycle.

7 Unfortunately the men couldn't put the fire out.

manage

Unfortunately the men _____ the fire out.

C A letter

Situation: There was a small fire last week in a block of flats in your street. *Write a short letter to a friend telling him or her what happened. Begin with these words: 'We had some excitement in our street last week.' (Just write the body of the letter, not the address, etc.)* 情景: 上周你住的街区的一栋公寓楼失火。给朋友写封信讲述失火的经过, 用指定的句子开头 (仅写信的主要内容, 不必写地址等) 。

_____

_____

_____

_____

_____

_____

_____

Lesson 20   Pioneer pilots

A   Comprehension

Read this passage and answer the questions below. Choose the best answer a, b, c or d for each. Answer the questions on the basis of what is <u>stated</u> or <u>implied</u> in the passage. 根据短文所述或暗指的内容选择正确答案。

THE WRIGHT BROTHERS

The first men in the world to fly and control a heavier-than-air flying machine were the American Wright Brothers, Wilbur and Orville. They began as bicycle manufacturers in 1892 and became interested in the possibility of flight, experimenting with gliders and kites for nearly ten years.

Then, on 17th December 1903, the brothers made history when they flew their plane for the first time on the beach at Kitty Hawk, North Carolina. They had spent a lot of time there studying the seabirds and the local people regarded them almost as a couple of idiots.

However, bearing in mind the information about bird flight, and of course their experiments with gliders and kites, they had built the muslin-covered *Flyer I* with its 12-horse-power engine and 40-foot wingspan. They dragged it on its truck to the top of a 100-foot sand dune called Kill Devil Hill. With a strong wind blowing around them they shook hands and Orville climbed into the plane, refusing to wear a coat because of the extra weight. The engine roared and with Wilbur steadying the wing tip, the *Flyer* rolled forward, and then took off – the first self-powered, controlled flying machine. That first flight only lasted twelve seconds, but it proved that the brothers' theories were right – and that their father was wrong. He had said, 'It is given only to God and angels to fly!'

They completed a series of flights and the longest successful overland flight was 852 feet and lasted 59 seconds. Within two years they had improved the machine enough to cover 24.5 miles in 38 minutes at Dayton, Ohio.

All that happened in America: it was another six years before Louis Bleriot became the first man to fly across the English Channel in his *No. XI*.

It was probably right that Orville Wright should be the first man to fly the plane he and his brother had built together. He was born on 19th August, 1871, and was younger than his brother Wilbur who was born in 1867. As a child he had been a prodigy – he repaired sewing machines at the age of 5, made and sold kites to his friends, and built a printing machine at the age of 13. Neither he nor his brother went to High School, and it is said that their teenage money-making ventures included collecting the bones of dead cows and selling them for fertilizer.

A sad addition to the story is that Orville also earned the doubtful honour of being the first pilot to kill one of his passengers, a man called Lieutenant Selfridge – although apparently Orville also injured himself badly at the same time.

1 Why did the Wright Brothers become famous?

   (*a*) They made kites and gliders.

   (*b*) They were the first men to fly.

   (*c*) They produced bicycles.

   (*d*) They were bird experts.

2 The local people of Kitty Hawk clearly thought the Wright Brothers were

   (*a*) ordinary bird watchers.

   (*b*) peculiar holidaymakers.

   (*c*) beachcombers.

   (*d*) slightly mad.

3 How did the brothers keep *Flyer I* steady before it took off?

(*a*) They kept in on the truck.

(*b*) Orville took his coat off.

(*c*) They held hands.

(*d*) Wilbur held the tip of one wing.

4 How long was it after the first short flight before a man flew for over half an hour?

(*a*) A few days.

(*b*) Twelve months.

(*c*) Two years.

(*d*) Six years.

5 According to the text it seems that Orville Wright

(*a*) was older than his brother.

(*b*) had been a very clever boy.

(*c*) was 13 years younger than Wilbur.

(*d*) once ran a fertilizer factory.

6 When did one of Orville's passengers die?

(*a*) In 1903.

(*b*) During the Dayton, Ohio flight.

(*c*) In 1905.

(*d*) We don't know.

B Key structures and Special difficulties: revision

Complete the second sentence (in each pair), using the word given, so that it has a similar meaning to the first sentence. You must use the word in bold. 用所给的黑体词完成以下句子，使每组中的两句话表达相似的意思。

1 I often think that I'd like to be able to fly a helicopter.

wish

I often _____ helicopter.

2 We would like you to buy the tickets for us.

rather

We _____ for us.

3 The plan was for us to take off at 6.00 in the morning.

supposed

We _____ morning.

4 He landed safely on the sea, so he wasn't drowned.

would

If _____ drowned.

5 He was a remarkable racing driver as well as a first class pilot.

but

Not only _____ also a first class pilot.

6 The Wright Brothers succeeded in beating Bleriot by six years.

managed

The Wright _____ six years.

7 Quite by chance I met an old school friend as I was leaving the shop.

happened

As I _____ old school friend.

41

Lesson 22　By heart

A　Key structures and Special difficulties

Read each sentence carefully. In each one, identify the one underlined word or phrase (A, B, C or D) that must be changed for the sentence to be correct. 圈出句子中错误的词或词组。

1　Lots of my friends <u>should</u> play jokes <u>on</u> me whenever I <u>played</u> a <u>part</u> in a school play.
　　　　　　　　　　　A　　　　　　　　B　　　　　　　　　　C　　　　　D

2　The play is <u>highly</u> successful: it <u>has been</u> <u>racing</u> for a month <u>at</u> our local theatre.
　　　　　　　　　A　　　　　　　　　　　B　　　　C　　　　　　　　　D

3　<u>Much to</u> my embarrassment, my mother <u>would</u> always <u>say</u> my boyfriends <u>about</u> my childhood.
　　A　　　　　　　　　　　　　　　　　B　　　　　　　C　　　　　　　　　D

4　The woman's necklace was <u>such</u> <u>precious</u> that <u>no</u> company was <u>prepared</u> to insure it.
　　　　　　　　　　　　　　A　　　B　　　　　C　　　　　　　D

5　A colleague of <u>mine</u> <u>suggested</u> that we <u>shall</u> all go <u>on strike</u> for more money.
　　　　　　　　A　　　B　　　　　　　　C　　　　　D

6　My grandfather always <u>used</u> say that it was <u>extremely</u> <u>rude</u> to point <u>at</u> someone.
　　　　　　　　　　　　A　　　　　　　　　　B　　　　C　　　　　D

B　Vocabulary

Each sentence has an underlined word or phrase from Lesson 22. Choose one of the words or phrases (a, b, c, d) which best keeps the meaning of the original sentence if it is substituted for the underlined word or phrase. Put a ring round a, b, c or d. 以下句子选自第 22 课课文。圈出与划线的词或词组最相近的答案。

1　There's nothing at all on this piece of paper. It's completely <u>blank</u>.
　　(a) empty　　　　　(b) unoccupied　　　　　(c) white　　　　　(d) free

2　It's getting very <u>dim</u> in here. Can you turn on the light, please?
　　(a) damp　　　　　(b) bare　　　　　(c) dark　　　　　(d) dismal

3　The teacher said she liked my composition, and then <u>proceeded</u> to criticize every line of it!
　　(a) continued　　　(b) finished　　　　(c) revealed　　　(d) enjoyed

4　I was once <u>cast as</u> an aristocrat in a play about the French Revolution.
　　(a) learned my lines　(b) given the role of　(c) saw a performance　(d) took part

5　My grandfather would sit for hours <u>on end</u> staring out of the window at the mountains.
　　(a) before nightfall　(b) continued　　　(c) without a break　　(d) outside

6　The singer's popularity <u>faltered</u> a few years ago, but it has picked up again recently.
　　(a) flickered　　　(b) faulted　　　　(c) flashed　　　　(d) weakened

44

C Comprehension

*Read this text. Six sentences have been removed from the text. Choose from the sentences **A-G** the one which you think best fits each gap (**1-6**). There is one extra sentence which you do not need to use. The first has been done as an example.* 选择方框中的句子填空，其中有一句是多余的。

THE PRISON PLAY

Reading the story about the actor who played a joke on one of his colleagues, I was reminded of one of those stories about plays performed by prisoners in prison.

The events took place in a prisoner-of-war camp in Germany during the Second World War. There were about 250 British and French soldiers and airmen in the camp, and as they had been imprisoned for so long, they had begun to write and perform plays and other shows. **1 / E** .

This particular prison camp wasn't like many other camps, however. **2 /.... .** It wasn't perhaps as bad as the Bastille in Paris, but it was a very old castle, and there were lots of tunnels and secret passages which the prisoners had found and which their German guards had not.

Since they had so much time on their hands, all of the amateur actors always managed to learn their lines by heart and it was extremely rare for anyone to falter. The play they were going to perform on this occasion had been specially written to involve as many men as possible. Almost all of them were given parts to play and lines to learn. This particular performance was extremely important. **3 / .... .** It allowed lots of the prisoners to assemble on the stage at one time but at the same time to hide quite easily from the audience.

The curtain went up on the first scene to reveal a dimly-lit bar in Chicago in the 1920s. **4 / .... .** As the play progressed, more and more men came onto the stage.

While three or four of the main characters were acting near the front of the stage, a crowd of the others stood or moved around the dimly-lit scenery behind. **5 / .... .** This was ideal because, while the play was going on, the prisoners were one by one climbing down a hole in the stage and crawling along a tunnel which led out under the perimeter fence to escape into a small wood some 500 metres from the stage of the 'theatre'.

6 / .... . Most of the men were caught within a kilometre of the fence and were bitterly disappointed, although two or three did manage to cover a few kilometres before they too were arrested. At least they enjoyed a certain amount of popularity with the other prisoners for a short time after their return.

A	The scenery was crude, but effective because there were so many bits.
B	Fifty men left the stage through the hole during the performance, but the mass escape was unsuccessful.
C	Because of this the Germans in the audience never saw exactly how many were on stage at any one time.
D	The German guards inspected the stage every day.
E	Prisoners and German gaolers alike would enjoy these regular performances.
F	Six gangsters were sitting round a table playing cards.
G	It was a castle.

Lesson 23　One man's meat is another man's poison

A　Vocabulary

Choose the correct word or words by putting a ring round a, b, c *or* d, *and write it or them in.* 圈出正确答案,并填在横线上。

1 There's no logic in that argument: it's completely _____.
  (*a*) logical　　　　(*b*) illogical　　　　(*c*) logistics　　　　(*d*) logician

2 They usually _____ a stroll in the garden after dinner.
  (*a*) go　　　　(*b*) make　　　　(*c*) do　　　　(*d*) take

3 I think the way that man eats his food is absolutely _____.
  (*a*) repulse　　　　(*b*) repulsed　　　　(*c*) repulsive　　　　(*d*) repulsing

4 She didn't want to, but she had to agree _____ that her brother was right.
  (*a*) reluctant　　　　(*b*) reluctantly　　　　(*c*) reluctance　　　　(*d*) more reluctant

5 When the girl left the dance late that night, she found to her _____ that her father was not there to meet her.
  (*a*) praise　　　　(*b*) dismay　　　　(*c*) shame　　　　(*d*) abuse

6 Our two cats _____ the sound of their metal dishes with mealtimes.
  (*a*) associate　　　　(*b*) combine　　　　(*c*) socialize　　　　(*d*) hear

B　Composition

Situation: 'One man's meat is another man's poison.' *What do you think? Write about 150 words about your own tastes in food and your attitude towards foreign food. Think of national dishes that are unusual, sweet, salty, raw, overcooked, etc. Tell us why you like them, but why perhaps a foreign visitor might not like them.* 情景:"萝卜青菜, 各有所爱"。你对这句话怎么想?用 150 个词描述一下你的口味和对国外食品的看法,选择一些不寻常的、甜的、咸的、生的或烹调过头的本国菜肴,告诉我们为什么你喜欢它们而有的外国游客则无法接受。

C Comprehension

Read this magazine article in which five English people talk about their taste in food. For items 1-10 below, choose from the people A-E. There are two answers to the last two questions, and the people may be chosen more than once. We have done item 1 for you. 根据每个人的口味选择人员，最后两题分别有两个答案，每个人可以多次选择。

My taste in food

Five people tell us about the food they like and the food they hate

A Joan Blackie

I like all kinds of food really – English and foreign. We often have Indian, Italian or Chinese food at home, but when I'm away on holiday, I always eat English food. My stomach turns at the thought of certain foreign food. Snails don't appeal to me, for example, and I've never tried them.

B Carol Carter

Whenever I go on holiday, in Britain or abroad, I always take a lot of my own food with me. I know it's silly, but I just like to stick to the food I know. Foreign food has never appealed to me. In fact, my stomach doesn't even like food from other parts of Great Britain! It's what you're used to, I suppose.

C Graham Whitefoot

For me, snails are a great delicacy! So is octopus, and steak and chips! And I like cakes, and very sweet puddings, and Italian ice cream …

Basically, I like all kinds of food, but any dish must be prepared well. Potatoes, for example, have received praise and abuse, but they're my favourite vegetables – if they're prepared well.

D Pat MacDonald

A huge number of people that I know go out to different kinds of restaurants to eat – Italian, Thai, Indian and Chinese, as well as English. And I do, too. Strangely enough I don't like French food very much. On a sudden impulse once I ordered snails in a French restaurant and then wished that I hadn't. I have never been able to look at them since then.

E Robert Bush

I happened to be in a Greek restaurant last year while we were on holiday and I just fancied the idea of octopus. My friends thought I was mad, but I really enjoyed it. People are right: it is a great delicacy. In fact there are no Greek dishes I don't enjoy now.

Which person

➢ regrets ever trying snails?   1   D

➢ has never eaten snails?   2 ……

➢ enjoys all Greek food?   3 ……

➢ wouldn't choose to go to a French restaurant now?   4 ……

➢ likes all kinds of food, as long as they're cooked well?   5 ……

➢ enjoyed octopus the first time he/she tried it?   6 ……

Which people

➢ like eating various foreign foods in England?   7 ……   8 ……

➢ always insist on eating English food wherever they are abroad?   9 ……   10 ……

Lesson 26   Wanted: a large biscuit tin

A   Key structures and Special difficulties

Each sentence below is incomplete. Beneath each sentence you will see four words or phrases (a, b, c, d). *Choose the one word or phrase that best completes the sentence. Put a ring round* a, b, c *or* d *and write in the word or phrase.* 圈出正确答案，并填在横线上。

1 Pat won't give you a lift to work, so it's no use _____ him.
  (*a*) will ask
  (*b*) to ask
  (*c*) asking
  (*d*) ask

2 _____ I would like to help you, I'm afraid I can't.
  (*a*) For
  (*b*) So as
  (*c*) A lot of
  (*d*) Much as

3 _____ the way, did Mary give you the eggs she promised me?
  (*a*) In
  (*b*) For
  (*c*) By
  (*d*) Up

4 Yesterday was an awful day for me: nothing _____ right.
  (*a*) did
  (*b*) turned
  (*c*) grew
  (*d*) went

5 The boy jumped out of the way of the lorry to avoid _____.
  (*a*) crushing
  (*b*) being crushed
  (*c*) be crushed
  (*d*) to be crushed

6 He offered me free insurance in an effort _____ me buy the car.
  (*a*) to make
  (*b*) of making
  (*c*) make
  (*d*) for making

7 The sailing boat was _____ weight that we used a crane to lift it.
  (*a*) so
  (*b*) such
  (*c*) such a
  (*d*) such an

8 Could you lend _____ $20 until tomorrow?
  (*a*) me
  (*b*) to me
  (*c*) for me
  (*d*) from me

B   Vocabulary

Read the text below. Then use the word given in capitals at the end of each line to form a word that fits in the space in the same line. 阅读短文，然后用所给词的正确形式填空。

It is generally accepted in the world of business that (1) _____   **ADVERTISE**
exerts considerable (2) _____ on the buying public, and that   **INFLUENCE**
clever (3) _____ influence different kinds of people in   **ADVERTISE**
different subtle ways. They do this by preying on our (4) _____   **WEAK**
What some (5) _____ seem to forget, however, is that   **MANUFACTURE**
they themselves (or their companies) have been (6) _____ in   **CLASS**

terms of what (7) _____ can be sold to them. Because **PRODUCE**
all companies are in (8) _____ with a number of **COMPETE**
others selling similar things, a (9) _____ amount of effort **COLOSSUS**
has to be put into every (10) _____ to campaigns launched **RESPOND**
by competitors. (11) _____ what your competitors will do next **ANTICIPATE**
is not easy, and (12) _____ new campaigns to sell a company's **DEVISE**
next range of goods provides full-time employment for a large number of people.

C Comprehension

Read each short text, the questions and the four possible answers. Choose the best answer to each question, a, b, c *or* d. 选择正确答案。

Text 1 (Instructions to students in a relaxation class)

You are so light that you are beginning to rise into the air. I want you to imagine flying over a beautiful green field on a magic carpet. You would like to go down and walk in the field, but much as you might like to, you can't. You just float in the air.

1 The students should feel so light that
   (*a*) they believe they can do magic.
   (*b*) they re walking across a field.
   (*c*) they think they are flying.

2 What can't the students do (apparently)?
   (*a*) Get back down to earth.
   (*b*) Float in the air.
   (*c*) Fly over the field.

Text 2 (The beginning of a talk)

Many of us who have made a close study of advertisements on television in recent years have come to the conclusion that they exert little influence on most viewers – with one important exception: young children. Advertisements have a tremendous effect on most children, so that they need little persuasion to beg their parents to buy what they have just seen on TV.

1 Who are still influenced by TV advertising?
   (*a*) Most viewers.
   (*b*) Young children.
   (*c*) Young parents.

2 How do advertisements influence children?
   (*a*) They make them want things.
   (*b*) They persuade them to talk to parents.
   (*c*) They make them buy TVs.

Text 3 (A public announcement)

We hope you enjoy visiting the different rooms in this new gallery of modern art. In order to make your visit even more enjoyable, we would like to invite visitors to enter our free competition to win a painting by one of our foremost contemporary artists.

1 What is the speaker doing?
   (*a*) Persuading people to come in.
   (*b*) Visiting one of the rooms.
   (*c*) Welcoming visitors to the gallery.

2 What can visitors win in the competition?
   (*a*) A second visit to the gallery.
   (*b*) A painting by a modern artist.
   (*c*) A free ticket for a friend.

Lesson 27   Nothing to sell and nothing to buy

A   Key structures and Special difficulties

Complete the second sentence (in each pair), using the word or words given, so that it has a similar meaning to the first sentence. You must use the word(s) in bold. 用所给的黑体词完成以下句子, 使每组中的两句话表达相似的意思。

1   It is said that that girl has a terrible temper.

   have

   That girl _____ terrible temper.

2   How many bags and suitcases have they brought just for the weekend?

   much

   How _____ for the weekend?

3   Sometimes John has wanted to give up everything and become a tramp.

   times

   There _____ become a tramp.

4   We set off early so that we wouldn't get caught in heavy traffic.

   so as

   We set off _____ heavy traffic.

5   Someone will have to do the whole job again.

   done

   The whole _____ again.

6   Do you know by whom this film music was written?

   who

   Do you _____ by?

7   The boys will have to sell the farm when their father dies.

   sold

   The farm _____ the boys' father dies.

8   In order to acquire more advanced computer skills Fred went to college evening classes.

   so that

   Fred _____ more advanced computer skills.

B   Vocabulary

Read this text, think which of the given words opposite best fits each space (a, b, c or d) *and write it in.* 圈出正确答案, 并填在横线上。

Real tramps like to think of themselves as 'gentlemen of the road', and not as beggars. But there are of course (1) _____ to the rule.

   A famous surgeon once passed a young man who was sitting on a pavement in London (2) _____. The young man stared at him hard. The surgeon, who was not a very kind man, looked at the young man with (3) _____ and said: 'If you look at every

54

(4) _____ the way you looked at me, you deserve to be poor. Others in your position have far more (5) _____. They don't become beggars asking people for money all the time.'

'I'm not asking you to feel (6) _____ for me,' the young man said to the surgeon. 'Don't (7) _____ me or people like me by your own standards. You might not believe it,' he continued, 'but I have (8) _____ chosen this way of life. I have (9) _____ comfort, a career, (10) _____ goods and the love of a family in order to lead the life I want. I am not a true beggar; I am a philosopher that begs.'

1	(a) competitions	(b) consequences	(c) acceptances	(d) exceptions
2	(a) persuading	(b) begging	(c) demanding	(d) asking
3	(a) contempt	(b) abuse	(c) impulse	(d) sneer
4	(a) traveller	(b) passer-by	(c) walker	(d) pectator
5	(a) good taste	(b) dignity	(c) pride	(d) behaviour
6	(a) envious	(b) aware	(c) sorry	(d) jealous
7	(a) judge	(b) estimate	(c) value	(d) esteem
8	(a) seemingly	(b) precisely	(c) deliberately	(d) greatly
9	(a) given	(b) sacrificed	(c) afflicted	(d) thrown
10	(a) comfortable	(b) proper	(c) real	(d) material

C Composition

Situation: Imagine you were a tramp for a day. *What was it like? Write 100-150 words describing the day. Tell us for example where you woke up, how you felt, what you had for breakfast, where you went, what you did during the day, and where you have planned to sleep tonight.* 情景: 想像你自己当了一天流浪汉。用 100 至 150 个词描述这一天的生活, 比如说: 你在哪里从睡梦中醒来, 你的感觉, 早餐吃什么, 去了什么地方, 一天中做了些什么, 晚上准备在哪里过夜。

_____

_____

_____

_____

_____

_____

_____

_____

_____

_____

Lesson 28　Five pounds too dear

A　Key structures and Special difficulties

Read each dialogue and the three possible responses. Choose the best response or addition to the dialogue, a, b *or* c, *and write it in.* 圈出正确答案，并填在横线上。

1　Woman:　No sooner had we left the ship than we were assailed by dozens of people selling things.

　　Man:　Yes, the way they behaved was absolutely outrageous!

　　You:　_____

　　(*a*)　That always happens on sailing ships.

　　(*b*)　So they attacked you before you left the ship.

　　(*c*)　But at least they waited until you had disembarked.

2　Student 1:　How long does it take you to get home from college?

　　Student 2:　Well, it usually takes me about half an hour.

　　Student 1:　_____

　　(*a*)　Oh, did it take longer yesterday then?

　　(*b*)　Did you take the bus this morning?

　　(*c*)　Will you take me with you?

3　Jane:　I bought this beautiful piece of silver in India.

　　Sue:　It is nice, isn't it? Is it handmade?

　　Jane:　_____

　　(*a*)　No, it wasn't made from copper.

　　(*b*)　Yes, it was made in India.

　　(*c*)　Well, it was made by hand as far as I know.

4　Woman:　The thief just grabbed my bag and ran off down the road.

　　Man:　What were you doing?

　　Woman:　_____

　　(*a*)　I chased him down the road, of course.

　　(*b*)　I had just taken some money out of my purse.

　　(*c*)　I was just chatting to a friend.

5　Harry:　No sooner had I given the man some money than he went off to the nearest café.

　　Peter:　What did you expect?

　　Harry:　_____

　　(*a*)　I thought he might have said thank you.

　　(*b*)　I waited till he came out of the café.

　　(*c*)　I was waiting for him to come back.

B　Comprehension

Read the text opposite, think of the word which best fits each space and write it in. Use only one word in each space. 选词填空，每个空仅填一个词。

UNCLE SILAS'S SILVER BARGAIN

Nobody likes to be thought a fool and people will go to great (1) _____ to conceal the embarrassing fact that someone has cheated them. (2) _____ this day my Uncle Silas is almost (3) _____ embarrassed to confess what happened to him.

You see, he once went to our local street market where tradesmen regularly (4) _____ the price of wares of all kinds. He really had no (5) _____ of buying anything at the market, but one stall was loaded (6) _____ silverware which looked good and which the stallholder admitted he was trying to get (7) _____ of. 'It's all good silver, sir,' said the man, 'but (8) _____ a favour to you, I'll let you have two pieces for the price of one.' Uncle Silas was impressed and began to (9) _____ closely much of the silver on display. Most of it wasn't as good (10) _____ the man said, but a candlestick looked excellent. He bought a small plate and was given a candlestick.

It wasn't (11) _____ he got home that he was able to look at his purchases carefully. After only a few second, Uncle Silas threw up his arms (12) _____ despair and shouted: 'I've been cheated by the oldest trick in the book. He showed me a genuine candlestick and then gave me a fake!'

C   A letter

Situation: You were on the same cruise liner as the writer of the text in Lesson 28 and wrote to an English-speaking friend. *Write the letter here (90-130 words) describing part of the cruise. Tell us for example where you went, what you did, what you saw, say something about the people you met and the mementos that you bought. Just write the body of the letter.* 情景: 你与第 28 课的作者同在一艘客轮上。给一位英语国家的朋友写信（90 至 130 个词）描述一下你的旅程，比如说，你去哪里，做了什么，见了什么，说了什么。说说你遇见的人和你买的纪念品。仅写信的主要部分。

_____

_____

_____

_____

_____

_____

_____

_____

Lesson 30   The death of a ghost

A   Vocabulary

Read the text below. Then use the word given in capitals at the end of each line to form a word that fits in the space in the same line. 阅读短文，然后用所给词的正确形式填空。

According to local tradition, the castle on the hill is (1) _____ to   **SUPPOSE**

be (2) _____ by the ghost of a soldier from the First World War.   **HAUNT**

Many of the (3) _____ claim to have seen him, and the local   **VILLAGE**

(4) _____ are happy to include it in tourist literature. A local   **AUTHORITY**

politician even referred to the ghost in a recent (5) _____. Some   **SPEAK**

people suspect that the 'ghost' soldier might be a (6) _____ who   **DESERT**

is being kept in (7) _____ in a room somewhere in the castle,   **HIDE**

but (8) _____ research has revealed nothing to support this   **CONSCIENCE**

theory. Personally, I would be (9) _____ if the ghost story were   **ASTONISH**

really true, but I feel (10) _____ to keep it alive for the sake of   **OBLIGE**

those who earn money by it. Anyway, would you be (11) _____ to   **WILL**

be accused of causing the (12) _____ of one of the major tourist   **DIE**

attractions in the area? I wouldn't!

B   Composition

Write the first paragraph (90-120 words) of a ghost story called 'Midnight'. Begin with the words 'The town hall clock struck midnight …' Tell the reader for example where the story took place, if there was a moon, if it was a quiet night or whether there was a storm, who was there and what happened. 写出一个名为"午夜"的鬼怪故事的第 1 段，用指定的句子开头。

_____

_____

_____

_____

_____

_____

_____

_____

_____

C Key structures and Special difficulties

Complete the second sentence (in each pair), using the word or words given, so that it has a similar meaning to the first sentence. You must use the word(s) in bold. 用所给的黑体词完成以下句子，使每组中的两句话表达相似的意思。

1 She said something really surprising to us.

told

She _____ surprising.

2 When he left for the last time, he said nothing.

goodbye

He didn't even _____ last time.

3 How many mistakes are there in your letter?

made

How many _____ your letter?

4 Do you think you could do something for me?

a favour

Do you think _____ ?

5 Frank should be in the office this afternoon.

supposed

Frank _____ afternoon.

6 Mr. Brown should have written to you last week.

supposed

Mr. Brown _____ last week.

7 When I was younger, I played football every Saturday.

used

I _____ younger.

8 The president was making a speech when we entered the hall.

speaking

The president _____ hall.

9 Isn't it about time you stopped smoking?

gave

Isn't it _____ smoking?

10 He didn't want to go to prison, so he refused to surrender to the police.

give himself

He wouldn't _____
_____ to prison.

Lesson 31   A lovable eccentric

A   Vocabulary

Each sentence has an underlined word or phrase from Lesson 31. Choose one of the words or phrases (a, b, c, d) which best keeps the meaning of the original sentence if it is substituted for the underlined word or phrase. Put a ring round a, b, c or d.

1 The captain of the ship completely disregarded the safety of his passengers.
   (*a*) noticed   (*b*) cared for   (*c*) ignored   (*d*) forgot

2 As a young man, my uncle was a very shrewd businessman.
   (*a*) conscious   (*b*) wise   (*c*) witty   (*d*) clever

3 Oscar Wilde was one of the most notable figures in London society in the 1890s.
   (*a*) people   (*b*) leaders   (*c*) eccentrics   (*d*) assistants

4 He is one of those men who dislike work intensely and will do anything to avoid it.
   (*a*) extremely   (*b*) very much   (*c*) severely   (*d*) a large amount

5 The man walked into the library and dumped a pile of books on the counter.
   (*a*) spread   (*b*) dropped   (*c*) gently put   (*d*) placed

6 Mary's boss reprimands her quite regularly for being late.
   (*a*) scolds   (*b*) blames   (*c*) tells   (*d*) criticizes

7 The authorities have drawn up an elaborate plan to combat increasing crime in the city.
   (a) a notable   (*b*) a careful   (*c*) an extraordinary   (d) a detailed

8 Don't worry about Mark: he invariably arrives at the very last minute.
   (*a*) regularly   (*b*) willingly   (*c*) largely   (*d*) occasionally

B   Key structures and Special difficulties

Read each sentence carefully. In each one, identify the one underlined word or phrase (A, B, C or D) that must be changed for the sentence to be correct.

1 Instead of serving me immediately, not one of the shop assistants drew any attention to me.
     A   B   C   D

2 The woman stepped out of the shop, onto the pavement and in the street without looking.
                        A   B   C   D

3 Would you mind my invite a friend to come to your party with me?
    A   B C   D

4 Can you imagine my to put any of my terrible paintings into the local art exhibition?
           A   B   C   D

5 Apart from be the wrong colour for me, the jacket just doesn't seem to fit properly.
    A   B   C   D

6 As she was such emotional and in tears, her friends insisted on her staying with them.
           A   B   C   D

C Comprehension

Read this text. Six sentences have been removed from the text. Choose from the sentences A-G the one which you think best fits each gap (1-6). There is one extra sentence which you do not need to use. The first has been done as an example.

A GREAT SPANISH ARTIST

Most people do not like to draw attention to themselves, which is probably why they find it difficult to understand eccentrics. After all, an eccentric is a person who draws attention to himself or herself by disregarding social conventions and the everyday dull routine that the majority of us simply get used to. **1 / C** .

Salvador Dali, the famous Spanish Surrealist painter, was not only a great artist, but was also an eccentric. Born on May 11 1904 in Figueras, Catalonia, he was, according to at least one source, apparently a nasty little boy who enjoyed beating his sister. **2 /.....** It is said that he also once took a bite out of a dead bat and that he was so despised in his hometown that the people stoned him in the streets. Who knows whether such stories are true? **3 / .....** What is also certain is that his paintings are elaborate, extraordinarily accurate, highly finished, and they sometimes appear to be deliberately sensational.

In 1928 he moved to Paris and joined the Surrealists. **4 /.....** He made a deep study of dream symbolism which he employed a great deal in his paintings. One of the most famous of his paintings is *The Persistence of Memory (1931)*. **5 /.....** The style of the painting – fluid watch faces draped over the edges of things – was recently copied in an advertisement for toothpaste. **6 /.....**

With the coming of the Second World War, Dali left Europe in 1940 and settled in the U.S.A,. later becoming a Roman Catholic and devoting his art to symbolic religious paintings. He died in 1989 and was buried in Figueras.

A	What is certain is that Dali's flamboyant style of dress and his curled moustache are legendary.
B	Commonly known as *Limp Watches,* it now hangs in the Museum of Modern Art, New York.
C	Has it ever occurred to you: If we were all eccentrics, there would be no social conventions to disregard, would there?
D	He quickly became one of the principal figures in the movement.
E	I can hardly imagine what Dali himself would have thought of that!
F	He was so shrewd he never allowed himself to be interviewed without a fee.
G	Whether he was reprimanded for this behaviour we don't know.

Lesson 32　A lost ship

A　Comprehension

Read each dialogue and the three possible responses. Choose the best response or addition to the dialogue, a, b or c, and write it in.

1　John:　　I hear they finally stopped searching for that old wreck.

　　Frank:　　Yes, I heard that, too. I wonder why.

　　John:　_____

　　(a)　I think they'd been looking in the wrong place.

　　(b)　What were they searching for?

　　(c)　They'd stopped before they found it.

2　Student 1: Mary was annoyed last week because someone told her that that pearl necklace of hers was valuable.

　　Student 2: Why was she annoyed then?

　　You:　_____

　　(a)　Because she'd better sell it.

　　(b)　So that she could sell it.

　　(c)　Because she'd only just sold it.

3　Woman:　　That company was fined £25,000 last month.

　　Man:　　But they only dumped some building rubbish in the corner of a field, didn't they?

　　You:　_____

　　(a)　Yes, they've dropped a lot of rubbish since last year.

　　(b)　Yes, but they'd been dumping rubbish there for months.

　　(c)　Well, they've been staging a protest for the past month.

B　Key structures and Special difficulties

Read each sentence carefully. In each one, identify the one underlined word or phrase (A, B, C or D) that must be changed for the sentence to be correct.

1　When I <u>answered</u> the phone, the caller asked <u>if</u> I <u>could</u> <u>receive</u> a message for my father.
　　　　　A　　　　　　　　　　　　　　　　B　　C　　D

2　James <u>has been</u> studying the subject <u>for</u> years <u>before</u> he really began to <u>understand</u> it.
　　　　　A　　　　　　　　　　　　　B　　　　　C　　　　　　　　　　　D

3　We <u>had</u> better invite him <u>to</u> come on the salvage operation, <u>else</u> he'll never forgive <u>us</u>.
　　　A　　　　　　　　　B　　　　　　　　　　　　　　　C　　　　　　　　　D

4　The teacher <u>suggested</u> that we <u>should</u> all wear old <u>cloth</u> as we were <u>likely</u> to get dirty.
　　　　　　　　　　A　　　　　　　　B　　　　　　　　C　　　　　　D

5　<u>While</u> you're upstairs, <u>would</u> you mind <u>taking</u> my book <u>from</u> my bedside table?
　　A　　　　　　　　　　B　　　　　　　　C　　　　　　　D

64

C Vocabulary

Read the text below. Then use the word given in capitals at the end of each line to form a word that fits in the space in the same line.

You wouldn't imagine the (1) _____ that we children felt when   **EXCITE**

we discovered an old chest in the attic in our grandparents' house. When we

finally opened it, we found that it was full of the (2) _____   **PERSON**

(3) _____ of one of our ancestors. We didn't know exactly who   **BELONG**

the original owner was, but from the (4) _____ of the chest – some   **CONTAIN**

clothes and personal papers – we gained the (5) _____ that he had   **IMPRESS**

been a (6) _____ captain. His uniform would have confirmed that,   **NAVY**

but it wasn't there. However, there were (7) _____ other articles   **NUMBER**

of (8) _____ which a gentleman, and possibly a seaman, would   **CLOTHE**

almost certainly have worn in the nineteenth century.

D A letter

Situation: In a recent letter, an English-speaking friend told you about a journey by boat. You want to tell him or her about a similar journey off the coast or down the river in your own country. *Write the letter here (100-150 words) describing the journey. Tell us for example how it began, what happened on the way and how it ended. Just write the body of the letter.* 情景: 在最近收到的一封来信中, 一位英语国家的朋友给你讲了他乘船的一次旅行。在回信中, 你想告诉他你在国内一次类似的经历。用 100 至 150 个词讲述一下你的旅程, 仅写信的正文部分。

_____

_____

_____

_____

_____

_____

_____

_____

_____

_____

_____

_____

_____

Lesson 33   A day to remember

A   Vocabulary

Read this text, think which of the given words below best fits each space (a, b, c *or* d) *and write it or them in.*

Panic on the Motorway

Most accidents are the direct result of some completely (1) _____ event, such as a phone ringing, or a bird flying through a window. Because it is so unexpected, the people who get involved often react with (2) _____.

My uncle was driving along a motorway last year when all of a (3) _____ a (4) _____ horse leapt over a fence and onto the carriageway into the path of oncoming traffic. Within seconds, even though most drivers were keeping (5) _____ on the car in front and in the other lanes, twenty cars had (6) _____ and the motorway began to resemble a wrecking yard. Every time one car came to rest, another would brake hard and (7) _____ into the back of it. (I've seen film footage of such accidents with, ironically, waltz music added.)

For at least a kilometre back down the motorway there was total (8) _____ and, as if this were not (9) _____, two kilometres farther back down the motorway, the traffic was at a complete standstill with no way for drivers to (10) _____ what was happening ahead.

1 (*a*) unforeseen   (*b*) hurried   (*c*) outrageous   (*d*) unconscious

2 (*a*) hurry   (*b*) catastrophe   (*c*) despair   (*d*) panic

3 (*a*) quick   (*b*) sudden   (*c*) hurry   (*d*) fast

4 (*a*) lost   (*b*) careless   (*c*) lonely   (*d*) stray

5 (*a*) a watch   (*b*) an eye   (*c*) a look   (*d*) a sight

6 (*a*) smashed   (*b*) hit   (*c*) bumped   (*d*) collided

7 (*a*) slide   (*b*) sweep up   (*c*) scour   (d) pull up

8 (*a*) confusion   (*b*) catastrophe   (*c*) mistake   (*d*) rush

9 (*a*) so   (*b*) besides   (*c*) just   (*d*) enough

10 (*a*) invent   (*b*) find   (*c*) discover   (*d*) inform

B   Key structures and Special difficulties

Complete the second sentence (in each pair), using the word or words given, so that it has a similar meaning to the first sentence. You must use the word(s) in bold.

1 He played too badly in the practice game to earn a place in the first team.
  enough
  He didn't _____ first team.

2 The cat pulled off the tablecloth and broke a glass vase.
   breaking
   The cat _____ in the process.

3 She had to brake very hard so as not to collide with the car in front.
   avoid
   She _____ the car in front.

4 Sue's boss spoke to her so harshly that he made her cry.
   reduced
   Sue's boss spoke _____ tears.

5 Why didn't Frank brake harder?
   should
   Frank _____ harder.

6 My grandfather has experienced pain and joy in his long life.
   experience
   My grandfather has _____ long life.

C Comprehension

Read this carefully. It's an extract from a letter. Some of the lines are correct, and some have a word which should not be there. If a line is correct, put a tick (✓) on the right. If a line has a word which should not be there, write the word in the space on the right. We have done the first two for you.

Last week was just a series of disasters, so I thought I would write and	✓
tell you all about it. First of all, you know there are animals that devour up	*up*
everything they can. Well, we've got a vacuum cleaner that's just like that.	(1) _____
Instead of sucking up just the dust and dirt from the carpets, besides ours	(2) _____
has also decided to try to suck up the carpet. So we had carpets with	(3) _____
holes in them and we decided to have some new carpet laid. I knew we	(4) _____
shouldn't have had done it. While the man was measuring for new carpets,	(5) _____
he slipped and smashed collided the window with his elbow. By the	(6) _____
time I called a man to come and replace the window, things were getting	(7) _____
out of control out. Of course there was broken glass on the floor and	(8) _____
the window man slipped and cut his hand very badly as he fell. There it	(9) _____
was rush hour as I drove him to the hospital, but the journey took up so	(10) _____
long that by the time we got there, the man had fainted!	

Lesson 34   A happy discovery

A   Comprehension

Read this passage and answer the questions below. Choose the best answer a, b, c *or* d *for each. Answer the questions on the basis of what is* <u>stated</u> *or* <u>implied</u> *in the passage.*

SENTIMENTAL VALUE

One of the most popular programmes on British television, with its regular following of dedicated viewers, is the *Antiques Roadshow*. Members of the public bring their cherished possessions along to a venue in their neighbourhood to be valued by antiques experts. Obviously the experts see a lot of assorted junk, but there are times when even the hardened professionals find it difficult to conceal their excitement on making an unexpected discovery. That brown paper bag that an old lady has brought to the table with something to be valued contains – yes – a rarity, a masterpiece, a superb piece of jewellery, ...

There was a time when antiques dealers and experts had a reputation for being a little pretentious – knowledgeable, but pretentious. That has changed, due partly to the influence of programmes like the *Antiques Roadshow*, and the experts now are bent on being as helpful as they can. I remember a conversation just like this in a recent programme:

'I suppose you'd like to know what it's worth,' said the expert, staring at a delicate bottle.

'Well, yes,' said the owner, adding, as expected, 'but naturally I wouldn't want to sell it. Sentimental value, you know.'

'Yes,' replied the expert. 'Anyway, as I said, it is very rare, and it's worth a mere £500.' And before the gasps of fascinated onlookers had died away, he added quickly, 'Of course, if it had been in perfect condition, it would have been worth ten times that – at least ten times.'

Such things make good television, if nothing else.

And then, within a few months, when all the fuss had died down, there was the bottle – a little perfume bottle, photographed in all its 'delicate' glory, to be included in the next sale of good European glass in a large London auction house. So much for sentimental value!

---

1 What do all the people bring when they come to the *Antiques Roadshow*?
   (*a*) Rarities and masterpieces.
   (*b*) A lot of junk.
   (*c*) Cherished and valuable antiques.
   (*d*) All kinds of old things.

2 How are antiques experts different now?
   (*a*) They won't talk to people as much.
   (*b*) They are very helpful.
   (*c*) They know less than they used to.
   (*d*) They are more pretentious.

3 'Sentimental value' is a value which
   (*a*) is purely practical.
   (*b*) is based on tender feelings alone.
   (*c*) an expert gives to an article.
   (*d*) is the true market value.

4 The bottle would probably have been worth £5,000 if it
   (*a*) had not been so unattractive.
   (*b*) had been signed by the maker.
   (*c*) had not been damaged somehow.
   (*d*) had been carved with a design.

5 In the last paragraph, the writer implies that people will nearly always be influenced by
   (*a*) money.
   (*b*) glory.
   (*c*) sentiment.
   (*d*) an auction.

B Key structures and Special difficulties

Read each sentence carefully. In each one, identify the one underlined word or phrase (A, B, C or D) that must be changed for the sentence to be correct.

1 Simon has <u>recently</u> <u>discovered</u> that he is <u>a just</u> 30 minutes older <u>than</u> his twin brother Frank.
            A   B   C   D

2 <u>Strolling</u> through the back streets, I <u>remarked</u> an old <u>junk</u> shop that I had never <u>been into</u>.
    A   B   C   D

3 As darkness <u>fell</u>, the <u>labyrinth</u> of cold corridors <u>became</u> even more <u>forbidden</u> than before.
          A   B   C   D

4 Fame and <u>fortune</u> seem to <u>expert</u> a particularly strange <u>fascination</u> on people <u>nowadays</u>.
          A   B   C   D

5 We had to <u>price</u> the lid <u>off</u> the tin with an old <u>dagger</u> because it was <u>rusty</u>.
          A   B   C   D

6 If you can pack all this <u>crockery</u> <u>carefully</u>, you will be <u>ample</u> rewarded <u>for</u> your trouble.
                       A   B   C   D

C Composition

Situation: Have you ever made 'a happy discovery' in a market or junk shop and bought something which turned out to be valuable? *Write a short account (120-150 words) of the incident, real or imaginary. Begin with the words: 'I once had an amazing piece of luck.' Tell the reader where you were, what you found, what happened – and what happened later.* 情景: 你曾经有过"幸运的发现"即在市场或旧货商店买到一件稀世珍品吗？ 用 120 至 150 个词描述一下你的经历（真实的或虚构的），用指定的句子开头。

_____

_____

_____

_____

_____

_____

_____

_____

_____

_____

Lesson 35   Justice was done

A   Comprehension

Read each short text, the questions and the four possible answers. Choose the best answer to each question, a, b, c *or* d.

Text 1 (A radio news item)

A magistrate in the north of the country has meted out justice in a perfect instance of making the punishment fit the crime. A man was found guilty of breaking into a junk shop in the town and sentenced. 'It serves you right,' the magistrate told the man. 'You wanted to know where everything was in the shop. Now's your chance to find out.' And with that he ordered him to spend a month tidying and cleaning the junk shop from top to bottom.

1 What did the man do?
   (*a*) He opened a shop in the north of the country.
   (*b*) He served a magistrate.
   (*c*) He broke into a junk shop.

2 How did the magistrate punish the man?
   (*a*) He made him tidy up the premises he had broken into.
   (*b*) He ordered him to serve in the shop.
   (*c*) He told him to list all the junk in the shop.

Text 2 (An advertisement)

The road to fame and fortune can be arduous – and many can't be bothered to devote the time and energy they should in order to become successful. They want it on a plate. But enrol in one of our 'Success In Life' courses and you could emerge as a new person. We can't convert you – but you can begin to convert yourself.

1 The speaker says that the road to fame is
   (*a*) usually successful.
   (*b*) hard and difficult.
   (*c*) fortunate.

2 If someone follows a 'Success In Life' course, he or she could
   (*a*) convert other people.
   (*b*) enrol for life.
   (*c*) become a different person.

Text 3 (Part of a lawyer's summary)

Ladies and gentlemen of the jury, now that you have heard the case for the prosecution, I will repeat that I do not believe that this young man is guilty of the crime which he has been accused of. But you have heard all the evidence and you must decide. Just bear in mind that it is the responsibility of the prosecution to prove beyond all reasonable doubt that he is guilty of robbery. Neither he nor the defence has to prove his innocence.

1 The speaker is almost certainly
   (*a*) the young man's defence lawyer.
   (*b*) the judge in the court.
   (*c*) the lawyer for the prosecution.

2 According to the speaker, the prosecution must prove a man's
   (*a*) evidence.
   (*b*) innocence.
   (*c*) guilt.

B Vocabulary

Read the text below. Then use the word given in capitals at the end of each line to form a word that fits in the space in the same line.

When I was a young boy, we lived close to a(n) (1) _____ factory.   **USE**

Because it was big and empty, how could we resist the (2) _____,   **TEMPT**

in spite of threats of (3) _____ to go and play in the place? If   **PUNISH**

anything, we were just (4) _____ or being adventurous. In our   **GUILT**

(5) _____ we never thought that anything would happen, but   **INNOCENT**

(6) _____ one day something did. One of my friends became   **EVENTUAL**

separated from the rest of us. We heard him calling, but his voice was just a

(7) _____ sound in the distance. The factory was huge, so we   **MUFFLE**

were (8) _____ to find him for a long time. When we did find   **ABLE**

him later, and without the (9) _____ of any adults, his face and   **INTERFERE**

hands were all (10) _____ from falling into a pile of coal.   **BLACK**

C Key structures and Special difficulties

Complete the second sentence (in each pair), using the word or words given, so that it has a similar meaning to the first sentence. You must use the word(s) in bold.

1 'Have you ever visited a court of law to watch a case?' she asked me.
wondered
She _____ case.

2 If they are at all doubtful about a man's guilt, a jury must acquit him.
have
A jury must acquit _____ his guilt.

3 The jury will reach a verdict and then the judge will pass sentence.
reached
The moment _____ sentence.

4 After we had put all our luggage in the boot of the car, we set off.
putting
We set off _____ car.

5 'I have been trapped down the hole for hours,' the boy said to his father.
that
The boy told _____ hours.

71

Lesson 36 A chance in a million

A Comprehension

This is part of a magazine article in which three English people talk about unusual coincidences. Read it. For items 1-8 below, choose from the people A-C. The people may be chosen more than once. There are two answers to the last question.

Amazing coincidences

Three people tell us about some odd coincidences – strange but true

A Tom Greenaway

'I never used to believe in coincidences,' says Tom Greenaway. 'I'm not normally credulous or gullible, but there was something strange about an experience I had recently. I was late leaving for work and was just about to get into my car when my wife called me. My boss wanted me to drop into another office on the way to work to pick up some important papers. The call only delayed me by five minutes, but it was enough. When I reached the office block to collect the papers, there wasn't much of it left. There had been an enormous explosion of some kind and dozens of people had been killed and injured. If I'd been there a little earlier … .' Then he added, 'It seems that circumstances do sometimes conspire to prevent accidents happening.'

B Pam Price

Pam Price says: 'My husband and I were touring in the north of England and stopped in an obscure little village. Before we left home, as usual I had bought a paperback to read. I didn't know the author and had never heard of the book. I was simply attracted by the cover. I was amazed that night, sitting up in bed, to find that the story was set in the very same village where we were staying. And we found that the novelist often stayed in the small hotel where we were. What are the chances of that happening, I wonder? People pour scorn on things like this, don't they? I would have a while ago, but not now.'

C Liz Chance

Recently Liz Chance discovered that she had a long-lost twin sister from whom she had been separated at the age of six months. When she and her sister Louise were reunited last year, they found incredibly that they had led almost parallel lives. 'We found that we had both married in 1995 and that we had both married a man called Ted: both Teds were antique dealers. We discovered that we are both keen on gardening and listening to jazz, and that we both live in a house in a road called New Road. I always knew something like this would happen.'

Which person

> chose a book to read on holiday almost by chance? 1 ……
> was reunited with a long-lost sister not long ago? 2 ……
> was somehow prevented from having an accident? 3 ……
> married an antique dealer? 4 ……
> thought that his or her life had been saved by a coincidence? 5 ……
> reads novels when he or she is away? 6 ……

Which two people didn't believe in coincidences until recently? 7 …… 8 ……

B   Vocabulary

Each sentence below is incomplete. Beneath each sentence you will see four words or phrases (a, b, c, d). Choose the one word or phrase that best completes the sentence. Put a ring round a, b, c *or* d *and write in the word or phrase.*

1 The terms of the contract were _____ unacceptable.
   (*a*) fully
   (*b*) amply
   (*c*) totally
   (*d*) intensely

2 I happily _____ the fact that I am wrong on this occasion.
   (*a*) except
   (*b*) agree
   (*c*) assume
   (*d*) accept

3 Whatever _____ that strange old woman who lived in your village?
   (*a*) occurred
   (*b*) became of
   (*c*) lived
   (*d*) happened

4 I was fully _____ with all the facts of the murder case.
   (*a*) related
   (*b*) presumed
   (*c*) acquainted
   (*d*) converted

5 The events in many science fiction films are _____ improbable.
   (*a*) wildly
   (*b*) fully
   (*c*) closely
   (*d*) sharply

6 There's a very _____ resemblance between you and Bill.
   (*a*) close
   (*b*) naive
   (*c*) straight
   (*d*) obscure

7 The man's story was so _____ no one believed it.
   (*a*) credible
   (*b*) incredible
   (*c*) credulous
   (*d*) incredulous

8 Many important changes in society have been _____ by necessity.
   (*a*) brought to
   (*b*) brought up
   (*c*) brought round
   (*d*) brought about

C   A letter

Situation: An English friend told you recently about an unusual coincidence that once happened to him or her. *Write part of a letter telling your friend about a similar coincidence. Write a short paragraph, saying where you were, what you were doing and what happened.* 情景：一位英国朋友最近向你讲了发生在他/她身上的巧事。写信告诉他/她一个类似的事件，仅写信的正文部分。

_____

_____

_____

_____

_____

_____

Lesson 37   The Westhaven Express.

A   Vocabulary

Each sentence has an underlined word or phrase from Lesson 37. Choose one of the words or phrases (a, b, c, d) *which best keeps the meaning of the original sentence if it is substituted for the underlined word or phrase. Put a ring round* a, b, c *or* d.

1 The express train went through the station with a mighty roar.
   (*a*) a strong　　　　(*b*) an influential　(*c*) a powerful　　　　(*d*) a long

2 'Come on, boys,' the teacher said to those at the back of the line. 'Stop dawdling!'
   (*a*) walking so slowly (*b*) chugging　　　(*c*) hitting each other (*d*) chatting

3 The old man lodged an official complaint about his neighbours' behaviour.
   (*a*) did　　　　　　(*b*) put　　　　　　(*c*) made　　　　　(*d*) set up

4 It was an exceptionally hot day for the time of year.
   (*a*) a totally　　　　(*b*) an unusually　(*c*) a fully　　　　　(*d*) an absolutely

5 He's never punctual for any appointments, so you can expect to have to wait.
   (*a*) temporary　　　(*b*) timely　　　　(*c*) first　　　　　(*d*) on time

6 People used to have an unshakable faith in their family doctor; no longer, I'm afraid.
   (*a*) a firm　　　　　(*b*) an exceptional (*c*) a naive　　　　(*d*) an improbable

7 Don't blame me if something goes wrong.
   (*a*) disapprove　　　(*b*) consult　　　　(*c*) conduct　　　　(*d*) criticize

8 It struck me as very odd that nobody mentioned how cold it was in the room.
   (*a*) Something hit me (*b*) I was consulted (*c*) It was surprising (*d*) I thought it

B   Key structures and Special difficulties

Read each sentence carefully. In each one, identify the one underlined word or phrase (A, B, C *or* D) *that must be changed for the sentence to be correct.*

1 While I was standing at the bus stop, the bus went straight passed without stopping.
   　 A　　　 B　　　　　　　　　　　　　　　　　　　　 C　　　　　　 D

2 Little he realized how much time his mother had spent washing his sports kit.
   　　　　 A　　　　　　 B　　　　　　　　　 C　　　 D

3 I couldn't help notice that you were consulting the timetable a few moments ago.
   　　　　　　 A　 B　　　　　　　　 C　　　　　　　　　　　　　　　　 D

4 Would you mind borrowing me $100 until the bank opens on Monday?
   　 A　　　　　　 B　　　　　　 C　　　　　 D

74

5 After a while it dawned <u>to</u> John that the timetable was <u>too</u> old <u>to</u> rely <u>on</u>.
                            A   B   C   D

6 They can't <u>stand</u> the thought of <u>cancel</u> the match, especially <u>as</u> it's <u>such</u> an important one.
           A   B   C   D

C   Comprehension

*Read this article about the life of a train driver. Choose from the list **A-F** (in the box below) the sentence which best summarises each paragraph (**Example** and **1-5**) of the article. There is an example at the beginning.*

A day in the life of a train driver
Peter Blake talks about his job

Example	**D**

When they leave school nowadays boys want to design computer games, fly jet fighters, or go into pop music. When I was a lad, all that any boys wanted to do was drive a train, and I was the same. That's why we used to spend Saturday mornings standing on a bridge over the railway line watching trains go up and down to London.

1	

I was first taught to drive a steam train. It was really hard work – not like driving an express diesel now. I had to learn how to shovel the coal into the fire to create the steam. It was hot and dirty, but there was also something romantic about those old trains.

2	

As a learner driver I was taught to keep calm and I have never once got into a panic, I'm glad to say. A bird once hit the windscreen of the train when I was travelling at 80 miles an hour. I kept calm, I didn't brake – which is what I might have done in a car. I got the train to the next station safely, but with a broken windscreen.

3	

I hate it when the service is dislocated – by bad weather, for example. As far as I'm concerned, the timetable has been designed for the benefit of the customers, and we should stick to it. It's not nice, but naturally the public blame us when trains are cancelled or delayed. I hate it even more when we are asked to go on strike, as we were last year.

4	

I really enjoy my work. There's nothing like driving an express train. From the moment I board the train to the moment we get to our destination, I enjoy every minute. Instead of chugging along at thirty miles an hour we often roar down the track at nearly 100 miles an hour. Of course I'm always aware of the safety of passengers, but travelling at high speed is *exciting*.

5	

I shouldn't really comment on the organization of the railways, but I think it's totally unacceptable that the system has been broken up into different regions and different companies. I often reflect how much better – and safer – the system would be if it were still a national state railway.

A	No accidents so far
B	The excitement of speed
C	Early days
D	<u>Every schoolboy's dream?</u>
E	One national railway
F	The timetable must be kept

Lesson 38   The first calendar

A   Comprehension

Read this text, think of the word which best fits each space and write it in. Use only one word in each space.

OUR MODERN CALENDAR

Many people wonder why the official income tax year in Great Britain starts on 5th April while the annual calendar begins on 1st January. And why do people born on 29th February have to cope (1) _____ having a birthday only once every four years? What accounts (2) _____ it? The aim of this brief article is to shed some light (3) _____ the matter.

The calendar which we use and rely (4) _____ today in most parts of the world is called the 'Gregorian calendar'. It (5) _____ introduced in 1582 by Pope Gregory XIII and is a modification (or reconstruction) of the previous Roman calendar. That calendar was (6) _____ the 'Julian calendar' and was a 12-month solar calendar introduced in 46 BC by Julius Caesar. It consisted (7) _____ 365 days, with an extra day every four years.

Although Pope Gregory (8) _____ already devised the system in the 16th century to cancel (9) _____ ten extra days accumulated by the Imperial Roman (or 'Julian') calendar, when Britain finally adopted the Gregorian calendar on 14th September, 1752, the country lost eleven days overnight. With the advent (10) _____ the new calendar came riots in the streets because people believed seriously that they (11) _____ lost time from their lives, and politicians (12) _____ attacked with cries of 'give us back our eleven days'.

Up to and including 1751, New Year's Day (13) _____ always been on 25th March. From September 1752, and with (14) _____ adoption of the new calendar, the New Year now began on 1st January. Eleven days were lost in September, and in 1753 not (15) _____ was 25th March no longer the New Year, but it immediately became 5th April – and that's (16) _____ the income tax year starts on that date.

B   Vocabulary

Read this text. Then use the word given in capitals at the end of each line to form a word that fits in the space in the same line.

I like history, but don't think I could ever have become a (1) _____.   **HISTORY**

76

I wouldn't have had the patience. From a (2) _____ collection **BEWILDER**

of facts, figures and often quite (3) _____ details, they work **SIGNIFY**

(4) _____ towards a picture of an era or a famous historical **STEADY**

character, on the (5) _____ that the picture will become clearer **ASSUME**

the more (6) _____ they have. **INFORM**

In the past people often had to make (7) _____ about their **DEDUCE**

forefathers based (8) _____ on a few written records together **SUB_**

with perhaps a (9) _____ of relevant artefacts, if they survived! **SELECT**

Contemporary (10) _____ of famous people have always been **PAINT**

valuable historical documents. Unfortunately, there are not so many pictures

of ordinary people in (11) _____, as it were. But such pictures as **ACT**

we have are often prized as much for their value as (12) _____ **SOCIETY**

documents as for their value as art.

C Composition

Situation: Imagine you are a historian in the year 2100 looking back at the twentieth century. *Write a short account or description (120-150 words) of one important event, one discovery or one person that had an impact on the world. Begin with the words: 'Perhaps the most important event / discovery / person in the 20th century was …' Tell the reader enough to make him or her want to find out more.* 情景: 想像你自己是一位生活在 2100 年的历史学家, 正在回顾 20 世纪。用 120 至 150 个词简要地描述一下对世界有影响的事件、发现或人物, 以激起读者的好奇心, 用指定的句子开头。

_____
_____
_____
_____
_____
_____
_____
_____
_____
_____
_____
_____
_____

Lesson 39 Nothing to worry about

A Key structures and Special difficulties

Complete the second sentence (in each pair), using the word or words given, so that it has a similar meaning to the first sentence. You must use the word(s) in bold.

1 I was so relieved to get out of that hot railway compartment!
   relief
   What _____ compartment!

2 We've had some terrible storms and rain this past month, haven't we?
   weather
   What _____ month!

3 Can you make him clean my car for me?
   get
   Can _____ for me?

4 'Is the man serious?' I kept wondering.
   was
   I kept _____.

5 'The petrol tank's empty,' the coach driver said to his passengers.
   told
   The coach driver _____.

6 'You should let me drive,' Mary suggested to us.
   that
   Mary suggested _____.

7 Has Jason recovered from that awful cold yet?
   got
   Has _____ yet?

8 How is Martha progressing in her new job?
   getting
   How _____ job?

9 'You must go to the hospital for some tests,' the doctor said firmly.
   insisted
   The doctor _____ tests.

10 It didn't matter what we said, he always did what he wanted.
    would
    No _____.

B   Vocabulary

Read this text, think which of the given words below best fits each space (a, b, c *or* d) *and write it in.*

AN AFRICAN CAR RALLY

When Charles and Bruce entered the African Car Rally, 2,000 miles of hard driving and obstacles, they did not underestimate what they had taken on. Most of the route was along (1) _____ roads covered with small stones, and pitted with holes while large boulders often marked corners. As they raced along, stones kept hammering (2) _____ on the underside of the car and they were very much afraid that one would puncture the petrol (3) _____.

It was a rough ride and they were always being (4) _____ up and down in their seats by the constant movement and were in danger of knocking their heads on the roof. They knew too that (5) _____ or later they would almost certainly have a problem with a wild animal. After all, this was Africa, and they were surrounded by them.

One day they stopped to rest and to (6) _____ the map, not because they were lost, but because they wanted to know what the large (7) _____ of water was that they could see in the distance to their right. Suddenly they saw a movement behind a (8) _____ of bushes. Then, before they had time to move, an animal (9) _____ at them. It was a huge rhinoceros. Luckily, it didn't reach them because for some strange reason, when it was about 20 metres away, it (10) _____ to one side and went on running in a different direction, finally (11) _____ to a halt a few hundred metres away.

To this day they have no idea why the rhino turned away from them and their car at the (12) _____ minute. Perhaps it was the colour of the car, or perhaps it just took pity on them! Who knows?

1 (a) cruel   (b) rough   (c) hard   (d) tough

2 (a) ominously   (b) angrily   (c) fully   (d) wildly

3 (a) bonnet   (b) boot   (c) gear   (d) tank

4 (a) leapt   (b) bumped   (c) moved   (d) jumped

5 (a) temporarily   (b) sooner   (c) rather   (d) earlier

6 (a) look   (b) watch   (c) consult   (d) glance

7 (a) stretch   (b) trail   (c) lot   (d) sea

8 (a) pile   (b) wood   (c) heap   (d) clump

9 (a) went   (b) flashed   (c) charged   (d) scooped

10 (a) ground   (b) swerved   (c) drove   (d) steered

11 (a) making   (b) going   (c) doing   (d) coming

12 (a) ultimate   (b) past   (c) final   (d) last

Lesson 40   Who's who

A   Key structures and Special difficulties

Each sentence has an underlined word or phrase. Choose one of the words or phrases (a, b, c, d) which best keeps the meaning of the original sentence if it is substituted for the underlined word or phrase. Put a ring round a, b, c or d.

1 As soon as we arrived at the campsite, we <u>erected</u> our tent.
   (*a*) put up　　　　(*b*) put out　　　　(*c*) put up with　　　(*d*) put off

2 The teacher couldn't <u>tolerate</u> the boy's bad behaviour any longer.
   (*a*) put up　　　　(*b*) put out　　　　(*c*) put up with　　　(*d*) put off

3 <u>Apart from</u> one or two minor mistakes, I thought the concert was excellent.
   (*a*) except　　　　(*b*) except for　　　(*c*) except from　　　(*d*) excepting

4 I woke at 6, got out of bed and <u>put on my clothes</u> immediately.
   (*a*) dressed　　　(*b*) dressed oneself (*c*) dressed up　　　(*d*) dressed in

5 The students <u>regarded</u> the lecturer with some interest as he demonstrated what they must do.
   (*a*) saw　　　　　(*b*) attended　　　(*c*) followed　　　　(*d*) watched

6 I know this is frustrating, but please try not to <u>lose your temper</u>.
   (*a*) behave stupidly (*b*) get impatient (*c*) become moody (*d*) get angry

7 It's no using trying to speak to her this morning: she's <u>in a mood</u>.
   (*a*) bad-tempered　(*b*) fierce　　　　(*c*) unhappy　　　　(*d*) very angry

8 'Don't <u>put the receiver down</u>,' the woman said into her phone. 'I *must* speak to you.'
   (*a*) hang on　　　(*b*) hang down　　(*c*) hang around　　(*d*) hang up

B   Vocabulary

Each sentence below is incomplete. Beneath each sentence you will see four words or phrases (a, b, c, d). Choose the one word or phrase that best completes the sentence. Put a ring round a, b, c or d and write in the word or phrase.

1 The authorities have _____ him permission to build a house on the land he bought.
   (*a*) permitted
   (*b*) presented
   (*c*) allowed
   (*d*) granted

2 They never seem to give us enough _____ warning of local roadworks.
   (*a*) advance
   (*b*) forward
   (*c*) before
   (*d*) progressive

3 I often think that _____ jokes can be cruel.

    (*a*) practice

    (*b*) practical

    (*c*) impractical

    (*d*) practicable

6 It's difficult to _____ Bob seriously: he's always telling jokes.

    (*a*) think

    (*b*) have

    (*c*) hear

    (*d*) take

4 We are sure the critic was speaking _____ when he called the painting 'the work of a genius'.

    (*a*) ironically

    (*b*) gratefully

    (*c*) ominously

    (*d*) naively

7 The team manager remonstrated _____ his team members about their behaviour.

    (*a*) at

    (*b*) for

    (*c*) to

    (*d*) with

5 They have just _____ a very silly joke on their friend.

    (*a*) done

    (*b*) had

    (*c*) made

    (*d*) played

8 Occasionally he indulges _____ a glass of whisky.

    (*a*) in

    (*b*) to

    (*c*) on

    (*d*) with

C A letter

Situation: The story in Lesson 40 reminds you of a hoax or practical joke that you once heard about. *Write part of a letter to an English-speaking friend describing the hoax or joke, real or imaginary. Just write a short paragraph (120-150 words) describing what happened.* 情景：第 40 课的故事使你想起了你听到过的一出恶作剧。用 120 至 150 个词向一位英语国家的朋友描述一下这出恶作剧（真实的或想像的），仅写信的正文部分。

_____

_____

_____

_____

_____

_____

_____

_____

_____

_____

_____

Lesson 41   Illusions of pastoral peace

A   Key structures and Special difficulties

Complete the second sentence (in each pair), using the word or words given, so that it has a similar meaning to the first sentence. You must use the word(s) in bold.

1 I can't understand why people extol the virtues of country living.
   beyond me
   Why people _____.

2 I just don't know where I'll be this time next year.
   something
   Where _____ know.

3 For most people that man's salary is a secret.
   earns
   How much _____ most people.

4 I'll never understand why girls go into raptures over that actor.
   something
   Why girls _____ understand.

5 I'm not concerned with what she told you.
   concern
   What she _____ me.

6 I'm not a bit interested in when our next exams are.
   interest
   When _____ a bit.

B   Vocabulary

Read this text. Then use the word given in capitals at the end of each line to form a word that fits in the space in the same line.

'It's surprising how (1) _____ it can be in the centre of the	**PEACE**
city,' an old (2) _____ said to me the other day. 'I know it's	**ACQUAINT**
(3) _____ impossible for you country people to understand us	**VIRTUAL**
city (4) _____, but just tell me this: why do you and your	**DWELL**
country friends (5) _____ refuse to believe that there is no	**OBSTINATE**
(6) _____ to be found in the centre of a city other than exotic	**PLEASE**
(7) _____ of all kinds? You know, within a few minutes' walk of	**ENTERTAIN**
almost any busy street in London there is a park full of (8) _____	**TWITTER**
birds. And such a (9) _____ of birds, too!'	**VARY**

C   Comprehension

Read this passage and answer the questions below.

GIVE ME THE COUNTRYSIDE ANY DAY

Part A

Many people in England go into raptures at the mere mention of the countryside. They regard the countryside as their own. It appeals to them as a natural birthright and, whether they could live there or not, they extol its virtues at every opportunity.

The sights and sounds of the countryside are what I love – green grass, trees and hedgerows, rivers and streams, hills and valleys, with herds of cows and sheep grazing peacefully. The whole of the countryside is so peaceful.

And the air, the clean air, so superior to the atmosphere in a town, which I find so dirty. And there is nothing like the sweet smell of new-mown hay or spring flowers.

Town and city people must sometimes wonder if descriptions of idyllic English country life are true or whether they are a hoax designed to put people off visiting the countryside.

Part B

I have to admit that all is not perfect in the countryside. Being a farmer or farm labourer, working the most unsociable working hours in any profession, must be a dubious privilege. Of all the sights and sounds in the country, the dawn chorus is one I could personally do without: birds all singing at 4 o'clock in the morning is no fun! From time to time too there is the unfriendly, but not unbearable, smell of dirty farmyards and crop fields recently sprayed with pesticides and other things. For young people there are few job opportunities and very little to do. But while the city lights glinting over the horizon might be attractive for a while, the attraction doesn't last long.

Ultimately, of course, the advantages far outweigh such drawbacks.

---

*Do the following statements agree with the views of the writer in **Part A** of the text? In the right-hand column write **YES** if the statement agrees with the writer; write **NO** if the statement contradicts the writer; write **NOT GIVEN** if it is impossible to say what the writer thinks about the statement.*

1 All English people would like to live in the country.   1 ....

2 The sights and sounds of the countryside are better than the town.   2 ....

3 The writer would never live anywhere but in the country.   3 ....

*Now choose the best answer for each of these multiple choice questions: a, b, c or d. Answer the questions on the basis of what is <u>stated</u> or <u>implied</u> in **Part B** of the passage.*

4 Which aspect of rural life does the writer dislike particularly?

   (*a*) Being a farm labourer.

   (*b*) Listening to the dawn chorus.

   (*c*) Spraying crops.

   (*d*) Employing young people.

5 The things the writer mentions in Part B might best be described as

   (*a*) regrettable disadvantages.

   (*b*) pastoral advantages.

   (*c*) unfortunate disasters.

   (*d*) dubious advantages.

Lesson 42   Modern cavemen

A   Vocabulary

Read this text, think which of the given words below best fits each space (a, b, c *or* d) *and write it in.*

MY FIRST POT-HOLING EXPEDITION

When a friend at school first asked if I would like to become a (1) _____ and explore a cave in the local hills the next weekend, I said yes. So the next Saturday I found myself in the hills with a group of men, all with this peculiar (2) _____ for 'climbing underground'. The men in the group were all experienced and taught me about the (3) _____ precautions to take before going underground. It was all a little like a (4) _____ operation. Check all your gear – boots, helmet, food and drink, ropes and rope ladders, safety first kit, and so on.

We (5) _____ into caving clothes in a small hut and then walked out into a field. In the rock at the bottom of a hollow in the field there was a (6) _____ about two feet wide and about three feet long. I followed the leader in and we began our (7) _____.

I had expected to experience an (8) _____ silence underground, but I was wrong. Apart from the noises we made, there was a constant noise of water dripping from the roof or from stalactites, or the sound of water running along under our feet.

My friends had told me that you often see small insects that (9) _____ in the dark, but I didn't see any. Anyway, as it was my first expedition and I had other things to worry about, I imagine such things would have been (10) _____ noticeable.

At one point we came to a wide stream about a metre deep. We had to (11) _____ across with the cold water up to our middles. Had the stream been any wider or deeper, of course, we would have had to use our (12) _____ rubber dinghy.

1	(a) caveman	(b) rambler	(c) pot-holer	(d) climber
2	(a) exploration	(b) illusion	(c) fascination	(d) deception
3	(a) necessary	(b) satisfactory	(c) precise	(d) relative
4	(a) a naval	(b) a military	(c) an army	(d) a militant
5	(a) dressed	(b) changed	(c) dressed up	(d) put on
6	(a) cavern	(b) rubble	(c) chasm	(d) fissure
7	(a) descent	(b) drop	(c) discovery	(d) downfall
8	(a) empty	(b) elaborate	(c) exotic	(d) eerie
9	(a) glint	(b) glow	(c) glisten	(d) glimpse
10	(a) virtually	(b) dimly	(c) hard	(d) barely
11	(a) plunge	(b) swim	(c) crawl	(d) wade
12	(a) pneumatic	(b) impressive	(c) inflatable	(d) explosive

B Key structures and Special difficulties

Complete the second sentence (in each pair), using the word or words given, so that it has a similar meaning to the first sentence. You must use the word(s) in bold.

1 We still haven't explored much of the ocean floor.
   remains
   Much of _____.

2 We only met because we went to the same party.
   might
   If we _____ met.

3 John found the entrance to the cave because he was looking for it.
   might
   Had he _____ cave.

4 If the scientists hadn't been so careful, they might never have discovered a cure for the disease.
   had not
   A cure _____.

5 They could hear a sound in the roof and they found that it was caused by two water pipes banging together.
   was found
   The sound _____ together.

C Composition

Write a short account (110-140 words) of the first time you tried a new sport or adventure activity (real or imaginary). Begin with the words: 'I shall never forget the day … .' Say why you took up the sport or activity, what happened when you started, how successful you were, and whether you are still doing it. 用 110 至 140 个词讲述一下你第一次尝试一种体育运动或一种探险活动的经历（真实的或虚构的）。用指定的句子开头。

_____
_____
_____
_____
_____
_____
_____
_____
_____

Lesson 43   Fully insured

A   Key structures and Special difficulties

Read each dialogue and the three possible responses. Choose the best response or addition to the dialogue, a, b *or* c, *and write it in.*

1 Woman: What happened to that old wrecked car on the corner of our street?
   Man: Oh, it was finally hauled away by the authorities.
   You: _____
   (a) Yes, I heard the council took it way.
   (b) So they ordered a recovery truck, did they?
   (c) What did the insurance company want it for?

2 Student 1: Have you heard? They've given us an extra week's holiday.
   Student 2: That's great! But why? I thought all the work had been done.
   Student 1: _____
   (a) Because the painting must be finished soon.
   (b) No, the redecorating still has to be finished.
   (c) The college has to be built.

3 Jane: Don't forget. The annual fete's on the last Saturday in August.
   Sue: No, I haven't forgotten. And it's bound to pour with rain on the day!
   You: _____
   (a) Why, is it held twice a year?
   (b) Why, did it rain last year?
   (c) Why, will we have to take our umbrellas?

4 Woman: If an insurance company thinks something is particularly risky, then you'll be obliged to pay quite a lot in insurance.
   Man: What does that mean?
   Woman: _____
   (a) It means: the greater the risk, the lower the premium
   (b) It means: the smaller the risk, the bigger the premium.
   (c) It means: the bigger the risk, the higher the premium.

5 Harry: Did they manage to salvage that ship that went down outside the harbour?
   Peter: Yes, they raised it sometime last week.
   Harry: _____
   (a) So it was launched last week, was it?
   (b) So it's been brought up then, has it?
   (c) So it'll be salvaged soon, will it?

B   Vocabulary

Opposite there are six sentences. Read them carefully. In each one, identify the one underlined word or phrase (A, B, C or D) that must be changed for the sentence to be correct.

1　The boy <u>dived</u> into the <u>canal</u> and didn't <u>arouse</u> to the <u>surface</u> for about three minutes.
　　　　　　　A　　　　　　　B　　　　　　　C　　　　　　D

2　They <u>put</u> so much <u>effort</u> into the open-air disco that they should have <u>assured</u> the event
　　　　　A　　　　　　B　　　　　　　　　　　　　　　　　　　　　　　　　C

　　<u>against</u> bad weather.
　　　D

3　It was so cold at the <u>garden party</u> that <u>guests</u> couldn't <u>help</u> <u>twittering</u>.
　　　　　　　　　　　　A　　　　　　　B　　　　　　C　　D

4　When the small boat was <u>hit</u> by the large <u>liner</u>, it <u>capsized</u> and <u>drowned</u> very quickly.
　　　　　　　　　　　　　A　　　　　　　B　　　　C　　　　　D

5　<u>Admittedly</u> now that Laura's thirteen she's <u>officially</u> a <u>teen</u>, but her parents don't want to
　　A　　　　　　　　　　　　　　　　　　B　　　C

　　<u>celebrate</u> the event!
　　　D

6　For one <u>agony</u> moment the woman stood <u>precariously</u> on the highest <u>point</u> of the bridge, and
　　　　　　A　　　　　　　　　　　　　　　B　　　　　　　　　　　C

　　then she <u>plunged</u> into the water.
　　　　　　　D

C　Comprehension

Read this text carefully. Read each statement below the text and tick whether you think it is true or false, according to what you have read in the text.

'Of course you can drive my car,' Tom told his friend Lee. 'I'm fully insured, and so are you.'

'Are you absolutely sure?' asked Lee. 'I'd like to see your insurance certificate.'

'All right,' said Tom, taking an official document out of his wallet, 'here's the certificate. Look, it says here – under "Who is entitled to drive under this policy?" – "Any person driving on the order of or with the permission of the policyholder."'

'And does that cover me?' asked Lee.

'Of course it does,' said Tom. 'You're being allowed to drive the car "with the permission of the policyholder", and that's me.'

'Fine,' said Lee and drove off at high speed. However, he had great difficulty in driving Tom's car and a few minutes later he smashed into a brick wall.

'I'm sorry,' said Lee, 'but it's all right. We can claim on your insurance, can't we?'

'No, we can't,' said Tom angrily. 'I'll deny that I ever gave you permission!'

		True	False
1	At first Lee doesn't think he will be insured to drive Tom's car.	……..	……..
2	Tom hasn't got an official insurance document with him.	……..	……..
3	The owner of the car can allow anyone to drive it.	……..	……..
4	Tom was prepared to admit he gave Lee permission to drive.	……..	……..

Lesson 44   Speed and comfort

A   Comprehension

Read this passage and answer the questions below.

'SO YOU STILL ENJOY FLYING, DO YOU?'

Part A

I have taken my last aeroplane flight. I have decided: I will not step into another passenger jet ever again. In spite of that, I have to admit that it is still the most civilized method of transport for long distances. It's smooth and effortless, and I can't deny how exhilarating the experience was looking down on the Swiss Alps on that last flight.

But the plane was stuffy, for 95% of the time the flight was monotonous, and inevitably the constant droning of the jet engines slowly lulled most other passengers and me to sleep.

However you decide to spend your time – and I tend to read most of the time – there isn't always something to keep you occupied, as there is on a cruise, for example. Of course the airlines have devised ways of keeping passengers awake and entertained: give them food and drink, give them a film, and let them listen to music. But it doesn't work for me, and I suspect that it doesn't always work for others, either.

Part B

And then there are the real problems of flying, not just the boring side of it. There are the dangers of being hijacked, of lightning striking the plane or of flying through a thunderstorm and suffering turbulence. Or an engine could burst into flames and we could crash into the sea. And what about air rage now – those passengers who suddenly become violent and can threaten the safety of the aircraft and everyone in it through their actions? Or what happens if the captain suffers a heart attack and can't fly the plane? Nothing can take my mind off these fears. – Or have I been watching too many disaster movies?

---

*Do the following statements agree with the views of the writer in **Part A** of the text? In the right-hand column write **YES** if the statement agrees with the writer; write **NO** if the statement contradicts the writer; write **NOT GIVEN** if it is impossible to say what the writer thinks about the statement.*

1 Flying is the most exhilarating form of travel.   1 ....
2 The noise in a jet aeroplane sends a lot of passengers to sleep.   2 ....
3 Many airlines provide books for passengers to read.   3 ....

*Now choose the best answer for each of these multiple choice questions: a, b, c or d. Answer the questions on the basis of what is <u>stated</u> or <u>implied</u> in **Part B** of the passage.*

4 According to the writer, what might make an aeroplane crash into the sea?

  (*a*) Hijackers.

  (*b*) A thunderstorm.

  (*c*) A violent passenger.

  (*d*) An engine catching fire.

5 Why does the writer wonder if he's seen too many disaster movies?

  (*a*) He suffers from air rage.

  (*b*) He has so many fears.

  (*c*) He doesn't worry about flying.

  (*d*) He has become hardened to accidents.

B Vocabulary

Read each dialogue, the question and the four possible answers. Choose the best answer to the question, a, b, c or d.

1 Man: This apartment's great, isn't it? I think we should take it.
   Woman: So do I. It's so spacious – not at all cramped!
   Why does the woman like the apartment?
   (a) It's very big.   (b) It's very clean.
   (c) It's got good ventilation.   (d) It's well decorated.

2 Karl: What are you doing for your holiday this year? Camping, same as last year?
   Peter: No, that's too exhausting. Something a lot more civilized. We've booked a cruise.
   Where will Peter and his wife spend their holiday?
   (a) On a train.   (b) On an island.
   (c) On a ship.   (d) On a campsite.

3 Mary: How did you get on in your interview?
   Dan: I can't say I positively enjoyed it, but at least I wasn't intimidated by the woman interviewer.
   How did Dan feel about the interviewer?
   (a) She confused him.   (b) He didn't like her.
   (c) She didn't frighten him.   (d) He liked her.

4 Student 1: Don't drink the medicine like that. You're supposed to sip it.
   Student 2: Oh, I thought it would be more effective like that.
   How are you supposed to drink the medicine?
   (a) Drink it hot.   (b) Take small mouthfuls.
   (c) Swallow it fast.   (d) Drink it from a spoon.

C A letter

Situation: You recently experienced a flight in a passenger jet aeroplane. *Write part of a letter to an English-speaking friend describing the flight, real or imaginary. Just write a short paragraph (110-140 words) saying what it was like and describing what happened.* 情景: 你最近曾乘喷气式客机旅行。 在给一位英语国家朋友的信中描述一下你的经历, 仅写信的正文部分 (110 至 140 个词)。

_____

_____

_____

_____

_____

_____

_____

Lesson 45   The power of the press

A   Key structures and Special difficulties

Complete the second sentence (in each pair), using the word or words given, so that it has a similar meaning to the first sentence. You must use the word(s) in bold.

1 An Italian football club offered the English player £2 million to move.
   was
   The English player _____.

2 Rebels have already overthrown the government in the new republic.
   by
   The government _____.

3 In any political system people can find it easy to abuse power.
   easily
   Power _____ system.

4 The first yachtsman to sail round the island will receive a prize.
   given
   A prize _____.

5 They are going to replace the old town hall by a brand new one.
   to be
   The old town hall _____
   one.

6 When the company became successful, we had to employ a public relations officer.
   as soon as
   A public relations officer _____
   successful.

7 To save the woman's life they flew a new heart 2,000 miles.
   flown
   A new heart _____.

8 They usually restrict entrance to the final match of the year to just 20,000 fans.
   generally
   Entrance _____ fans.

B   Vocabulary

Read this text. Then use the word given in capitals at the end of each line to form a word that fits in the space in the same line.

Newspapers and magazines are not only big enough to do enormous good, they
are also powerful and unthinking enough to cause (1) _____   **TELL**
   (2) _____. In a country like Britain, newspapers and magazines are   **SUFFER**

90

so concerned with their own press (3) _____ that it is extremely **FREE**

(4) _____ whether they have any feelings for the people they write **DOUBT**

about. This example should illustrate fairly (5) _____ what I mean. **DRAMA**

A year ago a man from London rose from (6) _____ when he won **OBSCURE**

£5 million on the national lottery. The win (7) _____ changed his **RADICAL**

life even though he tried very hard not to attract (8) _____ to **ATTEND**

himself. It was not so much the money as the (9) _____ and **PHOTOGRAPH**

(10) _____ phoning him all the time that made his life **REPORT**

unbearable. At least one magazine wanted (11) _____ rights to his **EXCLUDE**

story and never stopped phoning him or visiting his home to try to persuade him.

You might think that in a (12) _____ society an ordinary **DEMOCRACY**

individual would be able to demand as much (13) _____ **PRIVATE**

as anyone else. That is sadly not the case. The money did not bring the man

happiness and he became so depressed after a while that he committed suicide.

C   Comprehension

Read this short newspaper article, the questions and the four possible answers. Choose the best answer to each question, a, b, c *or* d.

While many small companies are struggling against terrible odds to survive in the present economic climate, one local company has refused to become another victim.

Dakota Trading, manufacturers of steel goods, with a staff of some 20 loyal employees, have the same pressing financial problems as many other companies, but in order to overcome them, they have brought about major changes.

A year ago they were still manufacturing chains, hawsers and other steel articles, as they had done for twenty years. Now, however, they have changed direction and are producing all kinds of plastic goods for garden parties and fetes.

1   Which of these would be the best headline for the article?
   (a)   Dakota Trading is victim of economic slump
   (b)   Local company refuses to change
   (c)   Dakota continue to manufacture steel
   (d)   Small company moves with the times

2   What does the Dakota Trading company do now?
   (a)   They rent chains, hawsers, etc. to building companies.
   (b)   They manufacture and sell plastic articles.
   (c)   They help local firms solve their financial problems.
   (d)   They sell chains, hawsers and other heavy equipment.

Lesson 46   Do it yourself

A   Vocabulary

Read these sentences carefully. They are all about do-it-yourself. In each one, identify the one underlined word or phrase (A, B, C or D) that must be changed for the sentence to be correct.

1 As a <u>novice</u> at <u>decorating</u>, he wishes he had never <u>embarked</u> <u>for</u> repapering the sitting room.
      A   B   C   D

2 The <u>publication</u> I bought had lots of <u>articles</u> about how to <u>fill</u> your <u>pleasure</u> time usefully.
       A   B   C   D

3 John was <u>proved</u> <u>wrong</u> again when a professional workman had to <u>put</u> things <u>correct</u> for him.
         A   B   C   D

4 When we tried to <u>reassemble</u> the engine we had <u>mishandled</u> earlier, nothing <u>seemed</u> to <u>fit</u>.
                  A   B   C   D

5 I'm a very <u>keen</u> do-it-yourself <u>enthusiast</u>, but I wouldn't <u>go</u> so <u>long</u> as to put in a new kitchen.
            A   B   C   D

6 I had to <u>please</u> <u>ignorance</u> when they asked me if I knew what to do with a <u>clogged</u> water <u>pipe</u>.
       A   B   C   D

7 He was not a born <u>handyman</u>, so he <u>called in</u> a professional <u>mechanic</u> to <u>install</u> the new bath.
               A   B   C   D

8 I was <u>doubtful</u>, but my wife insisted that the <u>mark</u> on the kitchen floor was a small <u>chunk</u> of
   A   B   C
oil from the lawn <u>mower</u>.
               D

B   Key structures and Special difficulties

Each sentence below is incomplete. Beneath each sentence you will see four words or phrases (a, b, c, d). Choose the one word or phrase that best completes the sentence. Put a ring round a, b, c or d and write in the word or phrase.

1 My mother said that she _____ fix the machine herself.
   (*a*) will
   (*b*) shall
   (*c*) had
   (*d*) would

2 The electrician wanted to know who _____ the lights.
   (*a*) repair
   (*b*) has repaired
   (*c*) is repairing
   (*d*) had repaired

3 She kept nagging and I wondered when I
_____ find time to mend the
vacuum cleaner.

(a) can

(b) was able

(c) could

(d) were able

4 I asked him how long the mower
_____ in the grass.

(a) had been rusting

(b) had rusted

(c) was rusting

(d) rusted

5 One day I will have to get round
_____ my bicycle.

(a) mend

(b) to mend

(c) mending

(d) to mending

6 The woman was very resourceful so, when
the lights fused, she said she
_____ any help.

(a) doesn't need

(b) didn't need

(c) hasn't needed

(d) hadn't needed

7 'I promise that I _____ your
washing machine as soon as I can.'

(a) repair

(b) will repair

(c) would repair

(d) may repair

8 We wondered if we _____
employ a professional carpenter after all.

(a) must

(b) will have to

(c) would have to

(d) had to

C Composition

*Write a short account (110-140 words) of the time you tried an unsuccessful do-it-yourself job
at home (real or imaginary). Begin with the words: 'That day everything went wrong.' Say what
job you decided to undertake and why, what happened when you started, what went wrong and
how you solved it in the end.* 用 110 至 140 个词讲述一下你在家里自己动手做却未能做成
功的一件事或一件东西（真实的或虚构的）。用指定的句子开头。

_____

_____

_____

_____

_____

_____

_____

_____

_____

_____

_____

Lesson 47   Too high a price?

A   Comprehension

Read this passage and answer the questions below.

FOOT-AND-MOUTH DISEASE: SOME OF THE FACTS

Part A

In 2001 the United Kingdom was hit again by foot-and-mouth disease, the first time since the 1960s, causing a national crisis. However, much of the panic and confusion was spread largely as a result of ignorance of the disease.

Foot-and-mouth is a highly contagious disease found in Africa, South America, Asia, the Middle East and parts of Europe. It affects cloven-footed domestic animals such as cows, pigs, sheep and goats, as well as wild animals like rats and deer and zoo animals such as elephants. Horses, however, cannot contract the disease.

It is very rare for humans to catch the disease. Indeed, only one case has been recorded in Great Britain and that was in 1967.

Part B

Foot-and-mouth disease is insidious and can be spread by direct or indirect contact with infected animals. The disease can be spread on the wind, and can also be spread by people, equipment or vehicles which have been in contact with the disease.

Although the authorities do not really know where this latest outbreak of the disease originated, it can enter a country in frozen meat imported from other countries where the disease is common. Unlike Mad Cow Disease (BSE) and the human equivalent CJD, foot-and-mouth has no implications for the human food chain. Any meat, milk, cheese and other dairy products can be consumed quite safely.

Part C

It seems that the only way to contain the disease is to kill infected animals. There is no cure for the disease, and although adult animals normally recover in 2-3 weeks, they sadly remain carriers of the virus for up to two years.

From the time the disease was first reported to the time the epidemic was officially declared over, a staggering one and a half million and more domestic animals were slaughtered and large areas of the countryside were closed to the public. These areas included parks, woods and forests, and various leisure attractions situated in the countryside.

---

*Do the following statements agree with the information given in **Part A** of the text? In the right-hand column write **YES** if the statement agrees with the text; write **NO** if the statement contradicts the text; write **NOT GIVEN** if the information in the statement is not given in the text.*

1   Foot-and-mouth hit the UK the last time a few decades ago.   1 ....

2   Foot-and-mouth disease can spread very rapidly.   2 ....

3   Horses can also be infected by foot-and-mouth.   3 ....

4   It is rare for cats and members of the cat family to catch the disease.   4 ....

*Now answer these questions on the basis of what is <u>stated</u> or <u>implied</u> in **Part B** of the text. Choose the best answer for each of these multiple choice questions: a, b, c or d.*

5 Foot-and-mouth disease is insidious because it is spread
   (a) by farmers and farm vehicles.
   (b) in so many different ways.
   (c) by being carried in the air
   (d) mainly by people who have been in contact with infected animals.

6 How is foot-and-mouth different from Mad Cow Disease?
   (a) It affects the human food chain.
   (b) People cannot consume dairy products
   (c) It is found in frozen meat.
   (d) Meat is still safe to eat.

*Choose one phrase (**A-D**) from the list of phrases on the right to complete each key point (**7-9** below) about **Part C** of the text. Write in the letter of the appropriate completion against items **7-9**. You do **not** need one of the phrases. (The information in the completed sentences should be an accurate summary of points made in the text.)*

Phrases

7 Infected animals have to be killed   ....
8 Thousands of animals had to be killed   ....
9 The public were not allowed   ....
   The phrase not needed is   ....

A because they carry the virus for 2 years.
B to visit parts of the countryside.
C during a 2-3 week period.
D to prevent the disease from spreading.

B Vocabulary

Read this text. Then use the word given in capitals at the end of each line to form a word that fits in the space in the same line.

The sheer volume of noise in a city centre nowadays is (1) _____   **STAGGER**

and for me personally it is the worst form of (2) _____.   **POLLUTE**

The worst (3) _____, I think, are large department stores,   **OFFEND**

where music blares out (4) _____ from speakers on the walls   **INCESSANT**

and in the ceilings, providing the ultimate (5) _____ to   **IRRITATE**

shoppers and making (6) _____ almost impossible. If pop   **CONVERSE**

music's only (7) _____ to modern life has been to add to   **CONTRIBUTE**

the volume of noise in (8) _____ life, then I'm glad I didn't   **DAY**

go into it as a profession. There is a pop song from the sixties or seventies

which is still played (9) _____ on the radio called 'Silence is   **REGULAR**

(10) _____'. I often wish we could hear more silence.   **GOLD**

Lesson 48   The silent village

A   Comprehension

*Read this article by a travel writer. Choose from the list **A-F** (in the box below) the sentence which best summarises each paragraph (**Example** and **1-5**) of the article. There is an example at the beginning.*

Travelling is my life

A travel writer for a famous magazine tells us a little about her life and profession

Example	C

I am very fortunate. I am now a much-travelled woman, but until I was 20 I had never been anywhere more remote than London. And coming from a country village in the far south I was struck by the architectural beauty of the capital. I understood immediately why foreign tourists descend on it in their thousands.

1	

The first time I travelled abroad was when I went over to France on a cross-Channel ferry. It was a school trip to Paris for a week, and I thought it was wonderful. The sights, the sounds, the smells, the language – they were all wonderful. I had never experienced anything like it, and the week had a profound effect on me. It gave me the travel bug!

2	

As a young girl I was always shy of strangers. I certainly had no plans to travel a lot. I left school and trained as a journalist on a local paper and somehow slowly began to concentrate on travel. I had a procession of jobs before I got this one with the magazine. Although I still write articles on other subjects, my main occupation now is writing travel and tourism.

3	

I can appreciate now why tourists go halfway across the world to visit a place. I was brought up in the vicinity of a major British tourist attraction, but never went there myself and couldn't understand foreign visitors. You read about something halfway across the world and want to see it for yourself. I remember that was just why I went walking in the Himalayas and looked up at Everest, and why I went on a strange but wonderful cruise in the Antarctic. You can read about a place, but it is totally different to be there, to see, feel, smell and hear everything yourself.

4	

Perhaps not surprisingly I have been to a lot of popular tourist resorts in Europe, Africa, the Far East and the West Indies, for example. But I like to try and find those unknown, inaccessible places – not only for myself, but also for people who want something different. Sometimes it's frightening. I remember visiting a village on the side of a steep hill in Bolivia where the inhabitants stood motionless as I walked in and didn't move until I walked out.

5	

The career of the previous travel writer on the magazine I work for now came to an abrupt end when he quite simply disappeared somewhere in South America. He was on a special journey and had told someone at his hotel that he had found a native to ferry him up a river to some remote villages in the jungle. Nothing has been heard from him since then. One day I'd like to try and find out what happened to him.

A	The tourist mentality
B	Always looking for the unexpected
C	A late developer
D	The road to being a travel writer
E	A sudden end to a career
F	The first taste of travel

B Vocabulary

Each sentence has an underlined word or phrase from Lesson 48. Choose one of the words or phrases (a, b, c, d) which best keeps the meaning of the original sentence if it is substituted for the underlined word or phrase. Put a ring round a, b, c or d.

1 Our holiday villa turned out to be a <u>dilapidated</u> old house.

(*a*) ruined   (*b*) forbidding   (*c*) deserted   (*d*) charming

2 In some of the most <u>inaccessible</u> villages people still fetch all their water from the stream.

(*a*) distant   (*b*) deserted   (*c*) remote   (*d*) unreachable

3 When she looked at the baby ten minutes after she had put him to bed, he was <u>fast</u> asleep.

(*a*) half   (*b*) hardly   (*c*) sound   (*d*) wide

4 People in villages are generally much more <u>hospitable</u> than city dwellers.

(*a*) tolerant   (*b*) polite   (*c*) unhealthy   (*d*) generous

5 Instead of shouting, the old man just <u>glared</u> at us and we knew we had done something wrong.

(*a*) peered curiously   (*b*) looked angrily   (*c*) glanced quickly   (*d*) glimpsed

6 When explorers first visited islands in the South Pacific, they were met by <u>hostile</u> warriors.

(*a*) angry   (*b*) helpful   (*c*) hospitable   (*d*) heroic

C A letter

Situation: You recently visited a famous place. *Write part of a letter to an English-speaking friend telling him/her about the place, real or imaginary. Just write a short paragraph (110-140 words) describing the place, where it is, what it was like and what impressed you most.* 情景: 最近你参观了一个著名的景点。 给一位英语国家的朋友写信, 给他/ 她讲讲这个景点(真实的或虚构的), 用 110 至 140 个词写一段话。

_____

_____

_____

_____

_____

_____

_____

_____

_____

_____

_____

_____

Lesson 49 The ideal servant

A Comprehension
Read each short text, the questions and the three possible answers. Choose the best answer to each question, a, b *or* c.

Text 1 (A radio or TV advertisement)
The days of domestic servants are long past. Most of us have to do the housework ourselves. But that doesn't mean we don't want to keep the things in our home clean from dust and dirt.   Are you still sentimentally attached to your old vacuum cleaner and your old furniture polish? Why not change to the new 'Presto', the combined vacuum cleaner and polisher? Just a few minutes every day – that's all it takes – and you could have gleaming floors and furniture.

1 According to the speaker, what do most of us still want to do?
  (*a*) Use our old vacuum cleaner.
  (*b*) Be sentimental about our home.
  (*c*) Have a clean home.

2 What does the new 'Presto' machine do?
  (*a*) It cleans furniture and floors.
  (*b*) It only polishes floors.
  (*c*) It makes glass gleam.

Text 2 (A news item)
A hotel maid who was dismissed from her post for 'airing her own views too often', according to the hotel owner, was today reinstated in her job at the 'Gables Hotel'. The maid had taken the hotel to court for unfair dismissal. The judge criticized what he called the 'fickleness' of the maid's employers and praised the young lady's industriousness. In their defence, the hotel owners said that the girl talked incessantly and persisted in giving her opinions to guests about all kinds of subjects, whether they wanted to hear them or not. The judge instructed the hotel owners to be more understanding in future.

1 The maid lost her job at the hotel because she
  (*a*) dried clothes in her room.
  (*b*) talked too much.
  (*c*) was fickle.

2 What did the judge order the hotel owners to do?
  (*a*) Talk to the girl.
  (*b*) Introduce the girl to guests.
  (*c*) Give the girl her job back.

Text 3 (Talk by a departmental head)
First of all, I want to congratulate you all on what we have achieved this month. The results for the department are excellent. However, the management has reluctantly come to the conclusion that the department will have to be reduced 50 percent by this time next year.
You may also have heard that Mr. Brown has left. I'm sorry to say he was discovered using the Internet for his own personal use and was dismissed instantly.

1 Although the department has done well,
  (*a*) they could do a lot better.
  (*b*) it is going to be cut in size.
  (*c*) they will miss Mr. Brown.

2 Why was Mr. Brown dismissed?
  (*a*) He only worked 50 percent of the time.
  (*b*) He was last to join the firm.
  (*c*) He used the Internet illegally.

B   Vocabulary

Read each sentence carefully. In each one, identify the one underlined word or phrase (A, B, C or D) that must be changed for the sentence to be correct.

1   To get the dry <u>mud</u> <u>off</u> those boots, you should <u>scrub</u> them very <u>hardly</u> with a stiff brush.
                   A B   C   D

2   I don't want to <u>illusion</u> you, but, that <u>parquet</u> floor is not real <u>wood</u>; it's <u>imitation</u>.
                          A   B   C   D

3   Kings and queens in the <u>past</u> always used to <u>entertain</u> their <u>guests</u> very <u>lavish</u>.
                              A   B   C   D

4   The police were <u>unrelenting</u> in their <u>search</u> for the <u>murder</u> of the <u>domestic</u> servant.
                     A   B   C   D

5   The museum <u>staff</u> polish the glass in the <u>display</u> <u>cabinets</u> so often that it is always
                        A   B   C
<u>glowing</u>.
  D

6   <u>No matters</u> where people <u>went</u> in the huge <u>rambling</u> house, they could always be <u>seen</u> on
    A   B   C   D
close circuit TV.

7   I don't think you need any <u>academic</u> <u>qualities</u> to be in <u>charge</u> of people <u>doing</u> housework.
                                  A   B   C   D

8   I <u>hardly</u> noticed the waiters in the <u>dining room</u>; it was almost <u>as if</u> they were <u>inaccessible</u>.
  A   B   C   D

9   As he <u>approached</u> into the room, the <u>drunk</u> almost <u>tripped</u> <u>over</u> a pot of paint.
          A   B   C D

10 The first job I was <u>expected</u> to do was to <u>snap</u> lots of <u>tins</u> of biscuits <u>neatly</u> in a corner.
                    A   B   C   D

11 As company <u>chairman</u>, my friend <u>reluctantly</u> had to preside <u>on</u> <u>monthly</u> finance meetings.
             A   B   C D

12 In the <u>procession</u> to the church all the children <u>worn</u> <u>immaculate</u> white suits or <u>dresses</u>.
       A   B   C   D

Lesson 50   New Year resolutions

A   Comprehension

Read this text about evening classes. Six sentences have been removed from the text. Choose from the sentences A-G the one which you think best fits each gap (1-6). There is one extra sentence which you do not need to use. The first has been done as an example.

ADULT EDUCATION EVENING CLASSES

Although people find nowadays that they have little time to do everything they want to do, and although they always seem to have a thousand and one jobs to do, many nevertheless find time to go to evening classes. **1 / F** .

Different education authorities in the UK have different schemes for adult students. **2 /**... . While some classes are for people who want to lay out their own garden, learn a foreign language, make simple furniture or put things right in the house, other classes aim to help people take exams in order to earn promotion at work or to get a different job. In other words, you can study to be a better handyman – or classes will help you qualify to be a professional carpenter, electrician, plumber or mechanic, for example. Obviously you usually have to take your own equipment to certain evening classes – tools and material, paintbrushes and the like. **3 /** ..... .

Adult education evening classes are an excellent idea, but there are pitfalls. One is that some people who enrol make the fundamental error of trying to do too much. So instead of taking on just one subject one evening a week, they take on three subjects, for example. And what happens? **4 /** ..... .

Sensible people compile a list of things that they will find useful in their career and things that they enjoy doing in their leisure time. **5 /** ..... . Anyone deciding to follow an evening course must be aware that they must follow it week in week out, not just go along whenever they feel like it – or when there's nothing better to watch on 'the telly' that evening! The trouble is, quite a lot of adults slip back into their old ways and miss lessons – just like they did when they were at school. **6 /** ..... . On the other hand, evening classes provide a valuable place to meet other people, and in fact some courses can be studied in conjunction with television programmes.

A Since the tuition fees are relatively low, however, few students mind such extras.

B Some of the lessons may not be as interesting as things on the TV screen.

C But however different the schemes may be, all classes aim at self-improvement.

D Then they match those interests or requirements with courses on offer.

E Like do-it-yourself, evening classes provide activities for older people.

F Evening classes are a common and popular form of ongoing education for people in work.

G Enthusiasm for at least one of the subjects quickly wanes, and they leave the course.

B Vocabulary

Read this text. Then use the word given in capitals at the end of each line to form a word that fits in the space in the same line.

I have just bought a formidable book (1) _____ *Tales of*   **TITLE**

(2) _____ *Men and Women*. I haven't read much of it yet,   **AMBITION**

but I am already finding it a little (3) _____, and I feel sure   **SETTLE**

it will prove to be my (4) _____. You see, as the title implies,   **DO**

the book is devoted to detailed accounts of the (5) _____   **ACCOMPLISH**

and (6) _____ of many famous people throughout history.   **ATTAIN**

The book is beginning to annoy me. Here I am, reading about the ambition

of famous people who, with monotonous (7) _____, have fought   **REGULAR**

against all odds and (8) _____ achieved their goals, and I am   **ASSIDUOUS**

just not like that – and nor are many of the other people I know. Like them,

I might make all kinds of (9) _____, but I can never keep them.   **RESOLVE**

I suppose if you resolve to fail, then (10) _____ is the result.   **FAIL**

C Composition

Situation: Someone you know (real or imaginary) is an inveterate smoker who desperately wants to give up. *In 120-150 words write what you might say to encourage him or her. Begin with the words: 'You know you can give up …' Say how he/she should approach giving up, what he/she should do and what he/she shouldn't do.* 情景：你认识一个烟瘾很大的人 (真实的或虚构的)，他/她正在拼命地试图戒烟。用 120 至 150 个词写一番鼓励他/她的话，用指定的句子开头。

_____

_____

_____

_____

_____

_____

_____

_____

_____

_____

Lesson 51   Predicting the future

A   Vocabulary

Choose the correct word by putting a ring round a, b, c *or* d, *and write it in.*

1 Compared with PCs today, early computers were extremely _____.
   (*a*) easy   (*b*) primitive   (*c*) rude   (*d*) simplified

2 There is little to _____ the boredom of waiting to see the doctor.
   (*a*) diminish   (*b*) resolve   (*c*) unsettle   (*d*) relieve

3 After a number of tests the doctors finally _____ the child's illness.
   (*a*) diagnosed   (*b*) foretold   (*c*) discovered   (*d*) predicted

4 It is _____ difficult for foreigners to learn to write Chinese.
   (*a*) fundamentally (*b*) assiduously (*c*) mentally   (*d*) notoriously

5 If he wasn't born in 1985, he was certainly born some time in the _____ 1980s.
   (*a*) middle   (*b*) centre   (*c*) mid   (*d*) average

6 To make the day out more interesting, we returned by an alternative _____.
   (*a*) route   (*b*) street   (*c*) road   (*d*) journey

7 What system does your PC _____ on?
   (*a*) trace   (*b*) recur   (*c*) trip   (*d*) run

8 Before we had computers, many office workers did _____, repetitive work.
   (*a*) dim   (*b*) bored   (*c*) dull   (*d*) unclear

9 I never dismiss a new _____ as unworkable until I have examined it in detail.
   (*a*) idea   (*b*) thought   (*c*) thinking   (*d*) opinion

10 I've heard they need a new sound _____ in the recording studio.
   (*a*) accountant   (*b*) mathematician (*c*) technician   (*d*) workman

B   Key structures

These dialogues use language from the Repetition Drills in Lessons 49, 50 and 51 of the teacher's book. Read each dialogue, the question and the four possible answers. Choose the best answer to the question, a, b, c *or* d.

1 (In a computer company)
Man: Are they checking the software today?
Woman: Not exactly, but it's being checked sometime soon.
Which of these statements is true?
   (*a*) The job will be done soon.   (*b*) The software has been checked.
   (*c*) Someone's checking the software now. (*d*) The job hasn't been done carefully.

2 Husband: I booked two seats for the theatre on Saturday.

Wife: I'd rather you hadn't done that.

What does the wife think?

(a) She wanted to go to the cinema.   (b) She is not happy her husband booked seats.

(c) She wanted to go to the theatre last week.   (d) She'd rather go to the theatre alone.

3 Boy: Was that your mother on the phone?

Girl: Yes, she said her train was late and asked if I could wait for her.

What did the girl's mother want her to do?

(a) Talk to her on the phone.   (b) Wait for her.

(c) Meet her off the train.   (d) Check the time of the train.

4 Woman: Is the job being done now?

Man: Yes, it is, but I'd rather they had waited for fine weather.

What is happening now?

(a) The people have finished doing a job.   (b) They are waiting for damp weather.

(c) The man is waiting for fine weather to do a job.(d) Some people are doing a job.

C   Comprehension

Read this text, think of the word which best fits each space and write it in. Use only one word in each space.

THE INTERNET

Computers have become more and (1) _____ common, so that in many homes in the world they seem to be as essential (2) _____ the oven and fridge in the kitchen or the TV set in the sitting room. (3) _____ Leon Bagrit might have foreseen a time (4) _____ computers would suggest to us alternative routes to avoid traffic jams, help doctors diagnose diseases or relieve office workers (5) _____ repetitive work, he could never have predicted the phenomenon which is (6) _____ such common use today – the Internet, commonly (7) _____ as 'the net'.

(8) _____ how relatively new the Internet is, it is amazing how rapidly it (9) _____ grown, and the number of different uses to which it is put is staggering. People consult websites for information, they send e-mails (10) _____ the world to each other, they advertise and buy and sell goods and services, and they can do all these things 24 hours (11) _____ day. We haven't had a computer at home (12) _____ very long, but we have already learned (13) _____ to use the Internet, and I spend lots of time on it.

I can't say that I have been completely taken (14) _____ by my PC, but it is trying very hard to rule my life!

Lesson 52   Mud is mud

A   Comprehension

Read this passage and answer the questions below. Choose the best answer a, b, c *or* d *for each. Answer the questions on the basis of what is* <u>stated</u> *or* <u>implied</u> *in the passage.*

A MEMORABLE SHORT STORY

The story of the green bottle of perfumed mud reminded me, for some odd reason, of a short story by the famous science fiction author, H. G. Wells. It may have been just the mention of the colour green, but it reminded me all the same.

The story, entitled *The Plattner Story* and published in 1896, tells how a teacher called Plattner in a private boys' school disappears for nine days after being 'blown up' in an explosion in the chemistry laboratory. One of the boys brought a little medicine bottle to class one day with some greenish powder in for Plattner to analyze. He was no chemist and had no idea what the substance was. It was when he tried lighting the powder with a match that the explosion occurred, and where Plattner had stood was simply space. He had disappeared!

At first Plattner was mildly annoyed and certainly a little puzzled to find himself in another world. He thought he was dead, and when one of the boys walked right through him, he stared in blank amazement. The world in which he found himself was bathed in an eerie light, like moonlight, and everything was tinted an unpleasant greyish green. He could see everything in the real world, but could hear nothing. And in the new place there were ghostlike figures.

The headmaster asked the staff to treat Plattner's strange disappearance discreetly, but even so the story got out. Some considered it a great joke; others didn't know what to think.

When Plattner finally returned, he made outrageous claims that he had been wandering in a different space, and evidently he had had an unusual experience of some kind. As if to dispel any doubts, he allowed himself to be examined medically and it was discovered that his internal organs had all been turned round: his heart now beat on his right side, and he could only write with his left hand from right to left. The state of his organs was permanent: they had not just been temporarily displaced. Plattner almost forgot how he had come into possession of the green powder until he was reminded of the boy who had brought it.

When prompted later to relate the story again or to explain what happened to him, he would decline politely and pretend to be too busy, and he apparently promised himself faithfully not to give any more chemistry lessons.

1 What made the writer of this passage remember the H.G. Wells story?
  (*a*) The mention of science fiction.
  (*b*) Plattner, the chemistry teacher.
  (*c*) The green bottle of perfumed mud.
  (*d*) The boy's medicine bottle.

2 Where did Plattner find himself after the explosion occurred?
  (*a*) In another room in the school.
  (*b*) On a place like the moon.
  (*c*) On the other side of the world.
  (*d*) In a strange world.

3 What proof was there that Plattner might have spent time in a different world?
  (*a*) His body organs had been displaced.
  (*b*) He had seen ghosts there.
  (*c*) The light in the place was unnatural.
  (*d*) A boy had walked through him.

4 Plattner decided to give no more chemistry lessons because he
  (*a*) was more interested in medicine.
  (*b*) didn't know enough about analysis.
  (*c*) didn't want the same thing to recur.
  (*d*) admitted he wasn't qualified.

B Vocabulary

Each sentence has an underlined word or phrase from Lesson 52. Choose one of the words or phrases (a, b, c, d) which best keeps the meaning of the original sentence if it is substituted for the underlined word or phrase. Put a ring round a, b, c or d.

1 The woman looked at me in <u>bewilderment</u> when I spoke to her in French.

   (*a*) doubt   (*b*) mystery   (*c*) horror   (*d*) confusion

2 The doctor gave me a strange <u>concoction</u> to drink and told me to go home and rest.

   (*a*) mixture   (*b*) recipe   (*c*) substance   (*d*) tablet

3 I hope this document will <u>dispel</u> any doubts you might have about the painting.

   (*a*) get rid of   (*b*) strengthen   (*c*) get out of   (*d*) dismiss

4 The man was fined for being <u>intoxicated</u> while driving a car.

   (*a*) tinted   (*b*) drunk   (*c*) embarrassed   (*d*) notorious

5 We thought the arrangement was <u>permanent</u>, but apparently it wasn't.

   (*a*) everlasting   (*b*) regular   (*c*) temporary   (*d*) full-time

6 The author's cousin Harry quite clearly had a rather <u>weird</u> sense of humour.

   (*a*) fanciful   (*b*) eerie   (*c*) strange   (*d*) outlandish

C A letter

Situation: You have invited an English-speaking friend to come to China and want to tell him/her about a few things to expect. *Write part of the letter telling him/her about a kind of shop that he/she might find unusual. Write a short paragraph (120-150 words) describing the shop, where it is, what they sell, how much you might have to pay for things, and so on.* 情景: 你已经邀请了一位英语国家的朋友来中国, 并想告诉他/她可能会遇到的一些事情。用 120 至 150 个词写封信向他/她描述一种他/她可能会觉得比较独特的商店。

_____

_____

_____

_____

_____

_____

_____

_____

_____

Lesson 53   In the public interest

A   Comprehension

This is part of a magazine article in which four English people talk about problems they have had with officials. Read it. For items 1-12 opposite, choose from the people A-D. The people may be chosen more than once. There are two answers each to the last three questions.

Do we need more ombudsmen?

Four people tell us what they think

A   Chris Hart

'We all need to be protected from high-handed public officials,' says Chris Hart, a local civil servant in his mid-20s. 'I am aware of it in my own job, and as an individual citizen.'

A year ago, Chris was unemployed and went to his local employment office to try to find work. While looking for a new job, many people can claim Unemployment Benefit. But not Chris. Because his previous employer failed to supply him with the correct form, an over-zealous local employment officer told Chris that he could not claim. 'Rules are rules,' the man said, and there was nothing he could do about it. When Chris tried to ascertain what the rules were, he met a blank wall.

'I feel cheated,' says Chris. 'I never obtained any real satisfaction or compensation. I would still like to lodge an official complaint, but I don't know how.'

B   Ann James

Ann James says: 'My elderly mother had a legitimate grievance against our local hospital. After a minor operation on her left arm, which was successful, a nurse or doctor forgot to give her prompt treatment when she complained of severe pain some hours later. As a result, she lost the use of her left hand. We were delighted when the health authority finally introduced a scheme through which grievances like hers can be investigated properly. We need an official government department or something to safeguard the interests of people like my mother. After all, not all old people have children to look after their interests.'

C   Lana Staines

Recently Lana, a mother of three, had a problem with the gas supply to her home. As they cook with gas and have gas central heating, the lack of supply was clearly important. 'The first thing I did,' she said, 'was to contact a suitably qualified gas fitter, who came, inspected our gas appliances and immediately suggested we contact the gas company. He didn't charge me for his time' After weeks of phone calls and correspondence, an official from the gas company finally came to see them, agreed there was a major fault, and agreed to dig up the pipes. The whole business had taken a month. 'What we need,' said Lana, 'is something like a Gas and Electricity Ombudsman. Of course there may be one, but information is difficult to get, and I think government departments are very secretive.'

D   Peter Chance

Peter Chance is an accountant who works for himself. He enjoys being self-employed and has about fifty clients, most of whom are also self-employed people.

A year ago one of his clients, a general builder, was prosecuted for cheating an old man out of £2,000. He was accused of pretending to be a professional roofer. He was of course totally incompetent and another roofing specialist had to re-do the job.

Peter's problem is that he has somehow or other been accused jointly with the man. The circumstances are rather complicated, but Peter maintains that he is innocent. He's also worried about the old man who ought to get some compensation. 'If only there were an Ombudsman to turn to,' he said.

Which person

- has clients of his or her own? 1 ......
- works for the government, local or national? 2 ......
- did not need to complain for himself or herself? 3 ......
- really needs help for another person as well as himself or herself? 4 ......
- actually quotes what a civil servant said? 5 ......
- made sure he or she got a qualified workman? 6 ......
- wrote a lot of letters to try and get a problem investigated? 7
- reported the introduction of one successful complaint scheme? 8 ......

Which people

- talk about the rights of elderly people? 9 ...... 10 ...
- would like to have contacted an Ombudsman? 11 ...... 12 ...

B Vocabulary

Read this text. Then use the word given in capitals at the end of each line to form a word that fits in the space in the same line.

Jack Brooks, a friend of mine, denies the (1) _____ that he is   **ACCUSE**

a professional complainer. Whenever he feels (2) _____   **SUITABLE**

justified, however, he will lodge a (3) _____ against any   **COMPLAIN**

public (4) _____ that he believes has treated him badly.   **OFFICE**

Jack loves getting involved in lengthy (5) _____.   **CORRESPOND**

He will write to the chief tax (6) _____ or the local health   **COLLECT**

(7) _____ pointing out strongly to both of them how   **INSPECT**

(8) _____ their staff are when he feels he has received poor   **COMPETENT**

service. At the same time, he is always a little (9) _____ about   **SECRET**

his complaining, because if his own boss were to discover what he does, he

would be (10) _____ reprimanded. After all, he is a civil   **SEVERE**

servant himself and actually works in a (11) _____ department   **PARLIAMENT**

dealing daily with (12) _____ from the general public.   **GRIEVE**

Lesson 54   Instinct or cleverness?

A   Comprehension

Read this passage and answer the questions below.

ANTS

Part A

There are few places on earth where you will not find insects. They constitute the largest and most diverse class of living creatures in the world, with approximately one million recognized species. Whether they fly, crawl or creep, or whether they are harmless, or dangerous, they can be strangely fascinating. A swarm of bees or wasps or locusts will fill some people with dread, a horde of ants will fill many with amazement.

What do all insects have in common? An insect's head typically bears a pair of feelers, or antennae, and a pair of compound eyes. An insect has six legs, each of the three body parts bearing a pair of legs, and the last two often bear a pair of wings each. Insects exhibit varied habits and are vitally important in different ways. Some, such as bees, pollinate plants, and some, such as locusts, are regarded as pests, while yet others, such as flies, mosquitoes and fleas, are carriers of diseases.

Part B

There are some 14,000 species of ant in the world. In biology the ant family is known by the Latin name 'Formicidae'. Ants are social insects which form (usually) permanent colonies in nests made in wood, soil, plant cavities or in other constructions such as houses. An ants' nest contains one or more fertile queens, many wingless sterile workers, and winged males that fertilize queens. Most ants scavenge animal remains. Some are predators, like the Amazon ants, which have jaws shaped to be used as weapons when raiding other nests. These ants depend on slaves of other ant species to run their nest and care for their young. Others feed on fungi, like the leafcutter ant that is found mostly in the New World tropics. And there are other specialists that live on seeds or honeydew, like the honey ant, whose colonies have special workers that have been adapted to store honeydew.

Part C

Ants have their own enemies, of course, and some have their own defence. The little red ant, for example, has a nasty sting containing formic acid. While this is effective against humans, however, it will not deter most birds or animals such as anteaters, particularly in Central and South America, which have a long snout and sticky tongue specially designed to eat ants and termites by the thousand.

And what picture do people have generally of ants? When I think of them, I immediately think of industrious creatures – cartoon ants forming enormous columns marching off to forage for food. (In reality, this cartoon picture is based on the army ant, a variety with small or no eyes and which does march in columns.) People also have a picture of extremely ingenious creatures all working together for a common good. Although they seem to be swarming around apparently aimlessly, just watch a horde of ants long enough and you will find signs of intelligence. Or is that semblance of order just instinct?

Do the following statements agree with the information given in **Part A** *of the text? In the right-hand column write* **YES** *if the statement agrees with the text; write* **NO** *if the statement contradicts the text; write* **NOT GIVEN** *if the information in the statement is not given.*

1   Insects outnumber all other living creatures in the world by 10 to 1.   1 ....

2   Most insects have compound eyes and antennae.   2 ....

3   Insects always have wings, even if they are difficult to see.   3 ....

4   Insects carry out a wide variety of tasks in nature.   4 ....

*Now answer these questions on the basis of what is <u>stated</u> or <u>implied</u> in **Part B** of the text.*
Choose the best answer for each of these multiple choice questions: a, b, c *or* d.

5 What makes us believe that ants are social
   insects?
   (*a*) There are so many species.
   (*b*) They create permanent homes.
   (*c*) There is one queen in a nest.
   (*d*) They make nests in houses.

6 How are Amazon ants different from
   leafcutter and honey ants?
   (*a*) They live in North America.
   (*b*) They do not form colonies.
   (*c*) They attack other ants.
   (*d*) They do not eat fungi

*Choose one phrase (**A-D**) from the list of phrases on the right to complete each key point (**7-9**
below) about **Part C** of the text. Write in the letter of the appropriate completion against
items 7-9. You do **not** need one of the phrases. (The information in the completed sentences
should be an accurate summary of points made in the text.)*

		Phrases
7 Formic acid will not help ants	....	A to help them find and eat ants.
8 Anteaters have a long nose	....	B to forage for food.
9 You must watch ants for a long time	....	C to protect them from anteaters.
The phrase not needed is	....	D to find any sign of intelligence.

B Vocabulary

Choose the correct word or words by putting a ring round a, b, c *or* d, *and write it or them in.*

1 Wasps have an _____ ability to 'smell' food miles away.
   (*a*) unnecessary   (*b*) unreasonable   (*c*) unpleasant   (*d*) uncanny

2 There's something wrong with this plant. The leaves are beginning to _____.
   (*a*) wane   (*b*) diminish   (*c*) wither   (*d*) fail

3 It took him a very long time to _____ the memory of the accident.
   (*a*) erase   (*b*) cut   (*c*) evolve   (*d*) alter

4 The girl screamed as a large _____ web brushed against her face.
   (*a*) moth's   (*b*) wasp's   (*c*) aphid's   (*d*) spider's

5 The man was watching the soldiers when, without any _____, they attacked
   him.
   (*a*) prediction   (*b*) prosecution   (*c*) pressure   (*d*) provocation

6 The horrific pictures from the battlefield filled me with _____.
   (*a*) revulsion   (*b*) dread   (*c*) illness   (*d*) revolt

7 As we switched on the cellar light, a large rat went _____ across the floor.
   (*a*) scurrying   (*b*) pouncing   (*c*) swarming   (*d*) crawling

8 Professional gardeners constantly wage _____ on insects and other pests.
   (*a*) attack   (*b*) fear   (*c*) battle   (*d*) war

Lesson 55   From the earth: greetings

A   Vocabulary

Choose the correct word or words by putting a ring round a, b, c *or* d, *and write it or them in.*

1 There are now many pieces of space debris _____ orbit around the earth.
   (*a*) in   (*b*) on   (*c*) at   (*d*) out of

2 Scientists have found no other planets capable _____ supporting life.
   (*a*) on   (*b*) to   (*c*) for   (*d*) of

3 Earth _____ the perfect conditions for life to evolve.
   (*a*) proved   (*b*) gave   (*c*) provided   (*d*) emitted

4 _____ present they have no vacancies for gardeners.
   (*a*) In   (*b*) On   (*c*) At   (*d*) For

5 There's something wrong with this oven: it's just not _____ enough heat.
   (*a*) emitting   (*b*) generating   (*c*) proving   (*d*) evolving

6 The machine was so delicate that when dust _____ got inside, it created a
major problem.
   (*a*) bacteria   (*b*) parts   (*c*) conditions   (*d*) particles

B   Key structures

*The following sentences use language from the Repetition Drills in Lessons 52, 53, 54 and 55 of
the teacher's book. Complete the second sentence (in each pair), using the word or words given,
so that it has a similar meaning to the first sentence. You must use the word(s) in bold.*

1   I didn't go to the concert because I couldn't get a ticket.
    able
    Had _____ concert.

2   Tom cleaned the car, so Sue didn't need to.
    have to
    Sue _____ it.

3   Someone must analyze a sample of that contaminated meat.
    analyzed
    We must _____.

4   You didn't slow down so you couldn't avoid the accident.
    if
    You could _____ down.

110

5   They made a stupid mistake because they didn't consider the problem carefully enough.

    such

    Had _____

    stupid mistake.

6   I didn't have to send John an e-mail because my secretary had already done it.

    so

    My secretary _____.

7   Can you get someone to clean the office windows by next Monday?

    cleaned

    Can you _____ next Monday?

8   He didn't shout, so she couldn't hear him.

    even if

    She wouldn't _____.

C   Composition

Do you think that we should continue to spend money on exploring space – either on going into space ourselves or searching for life elsewhere? In 130-170 words write what you think and give reasons why you think we should or should not continue with space exploration. 你是否认为我们应该继续在探索宇宙方面 —— 人类进入太空或在地球以外的地方寻找生命 —— 花钱?用 130 至 170 个词讲讲你的观点并解释一下你的理由。

_____

_____

_____

_____

_____

_____

_____

_____

_____

_____

_____

_____

_____

_____

_____

_____

Lesson 56   Our neighbour, the river

A   Comprehension

Read each short text, the questions and the three possible answers. Choose the best answer to each question, a, b *or* c.

Text 1 (A news report)

Four days of continuous rain are threatening to spell disaster for the village of East Ham and the many small farms in the vicinity. Situated on the River Avon, the village has often been flooded in the past, and villagers and farmers alike are used to watching the rising floodwater as the river overflows its banks. This time, however, local residents are particularly worried because the rain has been so heavy and has lasted so long. Not only do house owners face the prospect of losing their homes, it is clear that many farmers stand to lose their livelihood.

1   East Ham and the surrounding area are facing disaster because
(*a*)   the Avon has burst its banks.
(*b*)   it has often been flooded.
(*c*)   the rain has been so heavy.

2   Which people could go out of business?
(*a*)   A lot of residents.
(*b*)   Local farmers.
(*c*)   Many house owners.

Text 2 (Part of a talk by a village councillor)

I understand that some villagers are becoming unduly worried about the rise in the number of newcomers to the district. It is important to realize that a large proportion of these people are coming here to make a living: they aren't just going to commute to London and make no contribution to village life. I want to dispel any fears you may have by suggesting that eventually they will all play an important part in our village life.

1   Why are some villagers getting worried?
(*a*)   Other villagers are inviting newcomers into the village.
(*b*)   A lot of new people are coming to live in the village.
(*c*)   New commuters are going to take over parts of the village.

Text 3 (Part of a weather forecast)

Following the recent weeks of rain and unsettled weather, we can now look forward to a very dry period. This will be followed at the end of next week by a heat wave. Farmers in the south can now finally look forward to a harvest in good weather. We'd like to forecast good weather for the rest of the month, but with global warming and unusual changes in climate, it is proving more and more difficult to forecast with as much accuracy as we would like.

1   What's going to happen to the weather over the next week?
(*a*)   It's going to get a lot worse.
(*b*)   It's going to change dramatically.
(*c*)   It's going to be quite warm.

2   The forecaster apologized for not being able to
(*a*)   promise more showers.
(*b*)   deal with global warming.
(*c*)   predict the weather more accurately.

B Vocabulary

Each sentence has an underlined word or phrase from Lesson 56. Choose one of the words or phrases (a, b, c or d) which best keeps the meaning of the original sentence if it is substituted for the underlined word or phrase. Put a ring round a, b, c *or* d.

1 The kind of thing that happened last Saturday night is a regular <u>occurrence</u> in the village.

   (*a*) event   (*b*) presence   (*c*) development   (*d*) endeavour

2 The new dentist is much better than his <u>predecessor</u>.

   (*a*) his previous boss   (*b*) his ancestor   (*c*) the previous dentist   (*d*) his forefather

3 That fence over there forms the <u>boundary</u> between our garden and our neighbours'.

   (*a*) dividing line   (*b*) frontier   (*c*) border   (*d*) front

4 Thunderstorms at this time of year can <u>spell</u> disaster for farmers.

   (*a*) cause   (*b*) mean   (*c*) make   (*d*) prove

5 We weren't <u>unduly</u> worried when we didn't hear from Don for a week.

   (*a*) too   (*b*) rather   (*c*) quite   (*d*) fairly

6 Our friends keep two horses in the <u>meadow</u> behind their house.

   (*a*) grass   (*b*) orchard   (*c*) valley   (*d*) field

C A letter

Situation: An English-speaking friend has written telling you a little about a great river in his/ her country. *Write part of your reply in which you tell him/her about a great river in your country. Write a short paragraph (120-150 words) describing the river, how long it is, where it flows from, which part of the country, which towns or cities it flows through, and so on.* 情景: 一位英语国家的朋友写信给你, 谈及他/她们国家的一条大河。在回信中用 120 至 150 个 词描述一下你们国家的一条大河。

_____

_____

_____

_____

_____

_____

_____

_____

_____

Lesson 57   Back in the old country

A   Comprehension

Read this text, think of the word which best fits each space and write it in. Use only one word in each space.

ON THE MOUNTAIN

The plan had been forming gradually in Ben's mind. Peter had to die, and his death would be seen (1) _____ tragic accident. For hours, as they climbed, Ben became absorbed (2) _____ his own dark thoughts. Their combined objective was (3) _____ summit of the mountain: Ben's own objective was Peter's death. Although they (4) _____ made a comprehensive study of the mountain and the route, Ben was positive, (5) _____ neither of them had actually climbed it before, that the mountain was hardly familiar territory. Climbing up frozen rock was nothing (6) _____ studying a map down on the ground, as it were.

Some 300 metres below the summit they found, embedded (7) _____ the snow, the remains of a camp left (8) _____ the last climbers – a tattered tent and some provisions.

It was bitterly cold. After a few hours' rest, and (9) _____ wishing to carry any more equipment (10) _____ was necessary on the last stage of the climb, they left their own remaining provisions at the camp, and set off (11) _____ the summit. All went well until just before they reached the top, when the clouds rolled in and almost (12) _____ them abandon the climb. They could hardly see (13) _____, but they went on (14) _____ they reached the top. On the horizon they should have been able at least to glimpse the temple they had visited days (15) _____ on the way up, but they couldn't.

They stayed on the summit long enough to plant a flag and to (16) _____ photos. Then they started down, Ben insisting that Peter (17) _____ lead the way. About ten minutes later, when Ben saw Peter stumble some metres below him, he prayed he would fall, and was prepared to cut his rope (18) _____ that happened. Instead, Peter's voice echoed up the mountain: 'Be careful. I nearly fell. I'm fine now.'

Peter waited (19) _____ Ben to join him on the ledge below. Ben knew that this moment was critical. It had to be now and, whatever happened, Peter couldn't recover (20) _____ the fall. *This* accident had to be fatal.

B   Vocabulary

Read this text, think which of the given words below best fits each space (a, b, c or d) and write it in.

Although many young people (1) _____ their eighteenth birthday to be something special, and are disappointed when it turns out to be just another day, my own eighteenth birthday really was like an important (2) _____ in my life. It may sound amazing, but on that day I had an interview for a job (3) _____. A British company wanted school-leavers to join its operation in Australia. I wanted to go.

My father drove me to London, but there was no one at the interview itself to help me: I was on my (4) _____. I made a bad start, but (5) _____ I became more confident. I found many of the questions totally (6) _____, but somehow I still managed to (7) _____ through, and make a (8) _____ impression. I was nervous and the interviewer, who was a woman, wasn't at all (9) _____ by my bold answers and confident manner, but smiled politely at my answers. She seemed pleased when I said that I had always wanted to (10) _____ to Australia. (To be honest, I don't think I had ever considered it!)

When she started asking me about geography, I felt I was on more familiar (11) _____. She asked me the name of the largest man-made (12) _____ in the world and I (13) _____ to think for a moment. I didn't know the answer, and said I didn't, but I still got the job. It (14) _____ me so happy!

Oh, in case you're wondering, I no (15) _____ work for the company. I now have my own business helping other people who want to emigrate to Australia.

1 (*a*) expect	(*b*) look	(*c*) wait	(*d*) inspect
2 (*a*) kilometre	(*b*) milestone	(*c*) measurement	(*d*) milometer
3 (*a*) alien	(*b*) absent	(*c*) afloat	(*d*) abroad
4 (*a*) lonely	(*b*) solo	(*c*) own	(*d*) alone
5 (*a*) continually	(*b*) gradually	(*c*) usually	(*d*) alternatively
6 (*a*) comprehensible	(*b*) comprehensive	(*c*) incomprehensible	(*d*) uncomprehending
7 (*a*) stumble	(*b*) stroll	(*c*) scurry	(*d*) straggle
8 (*a*) negative	(*b*) neutral	(*c*) probable	(*d*) positive
9 (*a*) taken up	(*b*) taken in	(*c*) taken over	(*d*) taken to
10 (*a*) migrate	(*b*) immigrate	(*c*) emigrate	(*d*) alienate
11 (*a*) territory	(*b*) country	(*c*) land	(*d*) subject
12 (*a*) pond	(*b*) sea	(*c*) river	(*d*) reservoir
13 (*a*) gave up	(*b*) ceased	(*c*) put up	(*d*) stopped
14 (*a*) permitted	(*b*) made	(*c*) allowed	(*d*) let
15 (*a*) further	(*b*) sooner	(*c*) rather	(*d*) longer

Lesson 58   A spot of bother

A   Comprehension

Read this passage and answer the questions below. Choose the best answer a, b, c *or* d *for each.*
Answer the questions on the basis of what is <u>stated</u> *or* <u>implied</u> *in the passage.*

A MYSTERIOUS INTRUDER

When I unlocked the door and entered the study, I was met by a scene of utter confusion. I had established that there was no electricity, so could not switch on the ceiling lights, but even in the beam of my large torch, I could see that papers and books had been tossed all over the room and that drawers had been taken out and emptied. It was as clear as daylight to me that there had been an intruder, and not necessarily a thief. As I flashed my torch around the room, I spotted traces of red and sickly green on the walls and furniture, and I went cold. I was afraid that my new employers would reprimand me for being negligent in not locking all the doors and windows the previous night, but this was not my major fear. I thought that someone or something was still lurking in the room, watching my every movement.

As far as I could see, there was no trace of anyone having forced the door or of having opened any of the windows. It was weird. My employers were obviously not fussy people; they were no doubt veritable magpies in their own way, for even among the chaos I could see there was much that most people would normally have discarded. There were lots of brown paper bags, for example, little bits of string, bundles of rags, and old bunches of holly from past Christmases. It was a miracle there was room to put anything new into any of the drawers or cupboards. And there was an unpleasant odour that I could not identify.

I stood thinking: 'Whoever has done this thing must surely have entered by the window from the garden or used a skeleton key. There's something wrong here.' Then, on an impulse, I turned and flashed the light into the far corner of the room, and gasped. What I glimpsed there for just a second has given me nightmares ever since!

1 The writer used a torch because he
   (a) couldn't find the switch for the ceiling lights.
   (b) expected to find an intruder.
   (c) wasn't allowed to use the lights.
   (d) the electricity had failed.

2 Why did the writer 'go cold'?
   (a) He was frightened.
   (b) The window was still open.
   (c) He saw someone watching him.
   (d) Someone had clearly forced the door.

3 What was odd about the writer's new employers?
   (a) They never threw anything away.
   (b) They kept rags in paper bags.
   (c) They enjoyed Christmas.
   (d) They were smelly.

4 What must the writer have seen in the corner of the room?
   (a) A skeleton.
   (b) A flashing light.
   (c) Something horrible.
   (d) A monstrous creature.

B   Vocabulary

Read each sentence opposite carefully. In each one, identify the one underlined word or phrase (A, B, C or D) that must be changed for the sentence to be correct.

1 The man who <u>forgot</u> to lock the doors of the <u>factory</u> was accused <u>of</u> <u>negligent</u>.
                A   B   C   D

2 The <u>thiefs</u> not only <u>ransacked</u> all the bedrooms, they left the <u>rest</u> of the house in utter <u>chaos</u>.
   A   B   C   D

3 The actress <u>made</u> a terrible mistake in the first <u>scene</u>, but she quickly <u>regained</u> her <u>compose</u>.
          A   B   C   D

4 It was almost <u>inconceiving</u> how much <u>damage</u> the river <u>did</u> when it <u>overflowed</u>.
             A   B   C   D

5 With the sudden <u>discover</u> of some <u>fingerprints</u> <u>on</u> the door of the lift, the crime was <u>solved</u>.
              A   B   C   D

6 Our holiday <u>flat</u> was on the third <u>floor</u> and we could sit on the <u>basement</u> <u>overlooking</u> the sea.
           A   B   C   D

C Composition

Situation: How do you think you would react if you came back home to find that intruders had ransacked your home? *In 150-200 words write what you would do, what you would expect the police to do, and what punishment the culprits should receive if and when they were caught.* 情景：如果你回家后发现不速之客已把你的家里洗劫一空，你将作何反应？用 150 至 200 个词讲讲你准备怎么做，你希望警察做些什么，以及罪犯被抓后应受到什么样的惩罚。

_____

_____

_____

_____

_____

_____

_____

_____

_____

_____

_____

_____

Lesson 59   Collecting

A   Vocabulary

Read this text. Then use the word given in capitals at the end of each line to form a word that fits in the space in the same line.

Perhaps one of the most severe illnesses people suffer is (1) _____.   **BORE**

Tom and his wife Pat are (2) _____ and they claim that they are   **COLLECT**

never bored. For them, collecting is an (3) _____ part of their   **ESSENCE**

lives. As far as other people are concerned, it is quite (4) _____   **HARM**

because it doesn't hurt them, and it provides Tom and Pat with hours of

(5) _____.   **RELAX**

   Tom's main interest is first (6) _____ of early twentieth-   **EDIT**

century novels, and he already has a few that (7) _____   **LIKE MIND**

enthusiasts would die for. There is a remote (8) _____ that he   **POSSIBLE**

will acquire a new (9) _____ to his collection this week. It will   **ADD**

be an expensive (10) _____, but that doesn't worry him, and he   **ACQUIRE**

is (11) _____ confident to have the money ready.   **SUFFICIENT**

   Pat, on the other hand, (12) _____ avoids collecting books   **DELIBERATE**

in favour of small pieces of porcelain, which even many of her friends find

 (13) _____. But while some of them envy her for occupying   **DELIGHT**

her leisure time so (14) _____ , others still become annoyed   **CONSTRUCT**

when she talks of nothing else. That doesn't apply, of course, to the small

(15) _____ at which she and her husband are now often asked to   **GATHER**

give talks. At such meetings they have both become very popular.

B   Key structures and Special difficulties

These dialogues use language from Lesson 59. Read each dialogue, the question and the four possible answers. Choose the best answer to the question, a, b, c or d.

1 Man: Do you think Mary will ever be promoted manager of the store?
  Woman: Personally, I think the chances are pretty remote.
  What does the woman think about Mary?
  (*a*)   She will almost certainly become manager soon.
  (*b*)   She is very ambitious.
  (*c*)   She's not very likely to become manager.
  (*d*)   She will definitely never be manager.

2 Student 1: I think we ought to stay at home and study.

Student 2: Well, I'd rather do something more exciting.

What did the first student do?

(a) He suggested that they should stay home and study.

(b) He demanded to study.

(c) He recommended that his friend should study more.

(d) He insisted on staying at home.

3 Man: I may well become an expert on antique furniture, you know.

Woman: Possibly – if you study for a few years and work for a dealer.

What does the man think?

(a) He is going to be an antique furniture dealer.

(b) It is not very likely that he will be a furniture expert.

(c) He should work for an antiques dealer.

(d) It is quite likely he will become an expert on antique furniture.

4 John: Look at your room! I've never seen so much clutter! And loose bits of paper everywhere!

Karl: It's not that bad!

What is John criticizing about Karl's room?

(a) The filing system.

(b) The untidiness.

(c) The newspapers.

(d) The dust.

5 Bob: Look at this superb painting I bought today. It only cost £150 and the dealer said it was genuine. It's signed, you know.

Jane: Really? I think you should get someone to verify the signature.

What does Jane think about the painting?

(a) She doesn't think the dealer's opinion has any bearing on it.

(b) She has her doubts about its authenticity.

(c) She wishes she had bought it.

(d) She thinks it's terrific.

6 Woman: Look what I've bought! Another little toy.

Man: Not another one! I don't mind you collecting, but you're so indiscriminate!

What does the man think about the woman?

(a) She shouldn't collect toys.

(b) He doesn't like her collecting at all.

(c) He thinks she spends too much money on toys.

(d) She can't make sensible judgments about what she buys.

Lesson 60   Too early and too late

A   Comprehension

Read this passage and answer the questions opposite.

SOCIAL HABITS

Part A

Every human society has its own rules of behaviour. The sports club you belong to has its rules and regulations, as does your own family, your school or college class, or the country in which you live. Whether it is acceptable to cross your legs in public, whether you should or should not blow your nose in public, whether it is acceptable to sit or stand close to a person you are talking to, whether you should or should not shake hands on almost every meeting; these are all governed by the rules of the society we live in. But above and beyond that, the behaviour we all obey first of all is body language.

Body language is the use of bodily movements, signs and gestures to express our feelings, desires or intentions without using words. The rules that govern our body language play a vitally important role in our lives. These non-verbal signals and forms of communication can be a veritable minefield, and they are broken at one's peril.

Part B

It may well be relatively easy to explain the laws of a country to a foreign visitor. It is infinitely more difficult, however, even for an intellectual, a sociologist perhaps, to explain the rules of social behaviour governing what we should wear, how we should speak to different people in different circumstances, or how we should eat and drink. In some situations in the UK, for example, it would be unforgivable to wear a suit, whereas in many jobs you could not possibly wear jeans. Much of what we do, the way we act, is based originally on tradition, and how much deviation we will accept is to do with tolerance. We can understand why people are intolerant of unpunctuality. After all, time is the most valuable commodity we have, and to waste it seems a crime. It's more difficult to understand why some people are so intolerant of others wearing the wrong clothes. Neither native children nor foreign visitors are born with social customs like these, so both have to learn them.

Part C

We punish criminals who break the laws of a country. The results of disregarding even the most basic social customs of a community can be almost as serious, it seems to me. Doing or saying the wrong thing at the wrong time can spell disaster. While individuals who break the (often unwritten) rules of society are reproached for their rudeness, ignorance of dress code, unpunctuality, speaking with their mouth full, eating with their fingers, or whatever, they find themselves punished in other ways. Some find to their horror that they have not been promoted; others fail to get what they want. We may be tempted to ignore accepted social customs, but we all learn quite soon that rules cannot be broken without punishment. A bank employee who is adamant that he should be allowed to wear a T-shirt to work might be regarded by some colleagues as just an eccentric; others, however, will find his behaviour so unforgivable, according to custom, that somehow or other he will lose his job.

*Do the following statements agree with the view of the writer in **Part A** of the text? In the right-hand column write **YES** if the statement agrees with the writer's views; write **NO** if the statement contradicts the writer; write **NOT GIVEN** if it is impossible to say what the writer thinks about this.*

1 All human communities have the same rules of behaviour. 1 ....

2 Body language is not particularly important. 2 ....

3 Breaking the rules of body language can be dangerous. 3 ....

4 Most animal body language is not as advanced as man's. 4 ....

*Now answer these questions on the basis of what is <u>stated</u> or <u>implied</u> in **Parts B and C** of the text. Choose the best answer for each of these multiple choice questions:* a, b, c *or* d.

5 Where did the rules of social behaviour come from?
   (*a*) Sociologists wrote them.
   (*b*) Intolerant people created them.
   (*c*) We were all born with them.
   (*d*) They were formed from tradition.

6 How are social customs different from other human behaviour?
   (*a*) People acquire them naturally.
   (*b*) They are based on tolerance.
   (*c*) They have to be learned.
   (*d*) They are unnatural.

7 In what way can it be disastrous to disregard social customs?
   (*a*) A person can lose his/her job.
   (*b*) You can become a nuisance.
   (*c*) People can easily ignore you.
   (*d*) You will be called a criminal.

*Choose one title (**a-d**) from the list of suggested titles on the right to put at the head of each part of the text (**8-10** below). Write in the letter of the appropriate title against items **8-10**. One of the suggested titles is **not** needed. (Each chosen title should provide an accurate summary title of the part.)*

			Titles of parts
8	Part A	....	(*a*) SOCIAL CUSTOMS TO BE LEARNED
9	Part B	....	(*b*) SOCIAL HABITS AND CLASS
10	Part C	....	(*c*) THE IMPORTANCE OF BODY LANGUAGE
	The title not needed is	....	(*d*) BREAKING THE RULES

B   A letter

Situation: In his/her last letter an English-speaking friend told you a few things about social customs in the UK – how people behave. *Write a complete short letter in reply (about 200 words, with your address, date, etc.) describing some of the social customs that a foreign visitor should know about before visiting China. Remember particularly to point out those things that an English person should **not** do in order to avoid offending a Chinese host, hostess or business associate.* 情景: 在最近收到的一封信中, 一位英语国家的朋友描述了英国的一些社会习俗。用 200 个左右的词写一封完整的信, 讲一讲外国游客来中国前必须知道的一些中国习俗, 特别是一个英国人需要注意避免的事宜, 以免得罪主人、女主人或商业伙伴。

Workbook key

Lesson 1

A

2 The girl *told the man (that) a wild kangaroo had been spotted* in Regents Park.

3 When the girl said *she had seen a kangaroo, she knew she wasn't taken* seriously.

4 Descriptions *of the animal were given to the police* by lots of people.

5 No kangaroo *had been reported missing* from any local zoo.

B

1c When 2b wherever 3c unless 4b As soon as
5d As 6a and

C

1 to (in *discussing to who*) 2 Correct 3 about
(in *What about*) 4 To (in *To which*) 5 Correct 6 by
(in *by which*) 7 Correct 8 Correct

D

1c 2a 3d 4d

Lesson 2

A

1c He always goes over at this time to buy some milk.

2b Quite well, but he's always getting into trouble.

3c No, she's forever complaining about something.

4a Yes, he always goes out picking blackberries at this time of year.

5c Because she's constantly asking me for money.

B

1C 'by second thoughts' should be *on second thoughts* 2C 'to tears' should be *in tears* 3A 'At the times' should be *At times* 4D 'on debt' should be *in debt* 5B 'in the common' should be *in common* 6C 'at business' should be *on business*

C

1c start 2a sight 3b armed 4c going on 5a raise
6c cause

D (A possible answer)

When the vicar saw Bill in the light of his torch, he immediately asked him what he was doing there. Bill told the vicar that he had been trying to repair the bell and that he had been going up the tower every night for weeks. When he said he was hoping to give the vicar a surprise, the vicar said he had done that, and probably woken everyone in the village. However, the vicar was pleased, even when Bill told him the clock would always strike thirteen at one o'clock.

Lesson 3

A

1 rang 2 woke up 3 got 4 had 5 went 6 made
7 drank 8 ate 9 left 10 flew 11 stood 12 heard
13 thought 14 took 15 spoke 16 said 17 drove by
18 felt 19 began 20 told

B

1c narrow 2c history 3b remains 4a happened
5b preserved 6a decorated

C

1 colonial 2 prosperous 3 graceful 4 goddess
5 interesting 6 archaeologists 7 beautifully
8 discovery 9 civilization 10 drainage

D

1 has (in *has was explored*) 2 the (in *of the archaeologists*) 3 to (in *until to Roman*)
4 Correct 5 Correct 6 at (in *amazed at to find*)
7 at (in *she stood at*) 8 was (in *which was swept*)

Lesson 4

A

1a 2b 3c 4d 5d 6a

B

1 How long *has* Alf *been* a dustman?

2 *Have* you *been waiting* very long?

3 *Have* you just *bought* those overalls?

4 I *have drunk* two cups of coffee while I've been waiting!

5 Do you realize you *have been drinking* coffee all day?

6 *Have* you ever *visited* the U.S.A.?

C

1C 'anyone' should be *to anyone* 2D 'the police' should be *to the police* 3B 'told' should be *said* 4C 'uncovered' should be *discovered* 5D 'her' should be *to her* 6B 'the office manager' should be *to the office manager*

D (A possible answer)

Thank you for your letter which I have just received. I think you are very lucky. I haven't got a job yet, but I have been thinking about it.

I would like to become an archaeologist, but it is going to be difficult. I will have to take exams in history and one or two science subjects which I have been studying for the past three years.

You must write and tell me more about your new job soon. (79 words)

Lesson 5

A

1d had he forgotten 2c have I read 3d will you
meet 4b remembered 5b had she finished
6c did we realize 7d will you get 8a finished

B

Text 1: 1d 2d

Text 2: 1b 2d

Text 3: 1c 2b

C

1A 'Yangtze River' should be *The Yangtze
River* 2A 'an' should be *some* 3D 'latest news'
should be *the latest news* 4D 'Best way' should
be *The best way* 5A 'any' should be *some* 6D
'some' should be *the*

Lesson 6

A

1D 2A 3F 4C 5B

B

1 inaccurate 2 illegal 3 illegible 4 impatient
5 irresponsible 6 disagree 7 dishonest
8 dissatisfied 9 uncivilized 10 nonsense

C (A possible answer)

We never thought the raid would be so easy. Two
friends and I had planned a smash-and-grab raid
on a jeweller's shop in the arcade near Piccadilly.
It was after nine in the morning and the shops
were just opening. I drove our car down the
arcade with headlights on and the horn blaring,
and stopped outside the jeweller's. My friends
jumped out and smashed the window of the shop
with iron bars. When the owner and his staff
began throwing furniture out of the upstairs
window, one of my friends was struck by a heavy
statue, but he wasn't injured. In three minutes the
boys had taken everything they could carry and
scrambled back into the car. I put the car into gear
and we roared off down the road. (131 words)

Lesson 7

A

1c 2d 3b 4b 5d 6c 7c 8a 9c 10d

B

1d examined 2c paid 3c contained
4b has just rescued 5b was taking 6a got

C

1b 2c 3d

Lesson 8

A

1 d 2 c 3 a 4 b

B

1c wherever 2c where 3d Whatever 4a what
5c whenever 6c When 7b Whoever
8a whichever

C

1C 'since' should be *for* 2A 'going' should be
go 3A 'I'm decorating' should be *I've been
decorating* 4B 'been building' should be *have
been building* 5A 'have received' should be
received

Lesson 9

A

1 their 2 to 3 no 4 As 5 themselves 6 from
7 when *or* whenever 8 me 9 how 10 of
11 of *or* about 12 if *or* whether 13 being
14 likely 15 from 16 how 17 whose 18 up
19 everything 20 however

B

2 We had *such horrible weather* that we came
   home early.

3 My aunt's cat *is so affectionate* that everyone
   loves him.

4 John *is such an independent person* that he
   never listens to advice.

5 The men found *it so difficult to cross* the river
   that they had to turn back.

6 She *wears such fantastic jewellery* that
   everyone admires it.

C (A possible answer)

Dear Mary,

   I am writing to tell you unfortunately that I
will not be able to look after your cat Tom while
you are away on holiday after all.

   My mother has just phoned to tell me that my
father has been taken into hospital and that she
wants me to go and stay with her. I am so sorry
that I have let you down, but I know you will
understand.

   I hope you can get someone else to look after
Tom.

   All best wishes, (86 words)

Lesson 10

A

1d 2b 3a 4a 5d 6c

B

1c had jumped 2c had been injured
3a arrived 4a had been given 5b didn't rush

C

1 explanation 2 archaeologist 3 impression

4 ability 5 popularity 6 originality 7 journalist
8 responsibility 9 attraction 10 madness

Lesson 11
A

1b declare 2d unscrew 3c officious
4d tolerant 5a dreadful 6d smugglers

B

1C 'clear' should be *clearly* 2B 'confidently'
should be *confident* 3D 'guilty' should be
guiltily 4D 'encouraging' should be
encouragingly 5A 'honest' should be *honestly*
6A 'sarcastic' should be *sarcastically*

C

2 He *told me (that) he didn't* mind helping me.
3 The receptionist asked *us if/whether we
    wanted the porter to carry our* baggage.
4 The Customs officer asked *the man how much
    perfume there was* in his case.
5 Jim's mother *asked him where he had* been.

D (A possible answer)

I was on duty recently when a young man came
through the Green Channel and I thought he
looked like a smuggler. I asked him if he had
anything to declare and then asked him to unlock
his suitcase. While I was going through the things
in his case, I spotted a tiny bottle at the bottom of
the case. I thought it was perfume and
immediately accused the man of not declaring it.
He said it wasn't perfume, but some hair gel that
he mixed himself. When I unscrewed the cap to
smell it, it was very unpleasant and of course I
realized he was telling the truth. I put a chalk
mark on his case and told him he could go. (123
words)

Lesson 12
A

1 it 2 Correct 3 with 4 the 5 the (in *the wretched*)
6 for 7 enough 8 Correct 9 any (in *any water*)
10 plenty

B

2 If only I *were not short (I'd be a lot happier)*!
3 I wish I *had been (more) polite* to Mr. Smith
   yesterday.
4 If only *I hadn't eaten so much* lobster last
   night!
5 I wish *she would study harder*.

C

1c genuinely 2b death 3d spend 4d opportunity
5c boat 6c paradise 7d injured 8a trip
9c wretched 10d rescued

D (A possible answer)

HELP! My name is … and I have been
shipwrecked on a small desert island somewhere
in the Indian Ocean. I have been on this coral
island since the ship I was travelling in sank a
month ago. I have a rubber dinghy, a spear gun
and other tools, so I am surviving. But paradise is
boring! THIS IS NOT A JOKE. I really have been
SHIPWRECKED on a DESERT ISLAND!
PLEASE RESCUE ME!   (74 words)

Lesson 13
A

1b No, you needn't type them all today.
2a Yes, she must be at least 21.
3a Yes, there was, and I had to stop at every set
    of traffic lights.
4c Well, I didn't have to, but I thought they
    would like to see me.
5a Yes, everyone has to. It's a fancy-dress party.
6b They mean you mustn't park there.
7b Because we'll have to cover the furniture
    while we're decorating.

B

1c 2b 3c 4a 5c

C

2 I was *delighted to hear your* news.
3 We were *quite shocked to learn* about her
   illness.
4 'I am so *pleased to be here* this evening,' the
   speaker said.
5 Mary was *very/extremely sorry to learn of the
   death* of her dear friend.
6 John was *glad to be able to help* organize the
   party.

Lesson 14
A

1d 2b 3c 4c

B

1c made 2b put 3c have 4a pay 5b given
6a made 7d made

C

1c No, I'd rather you waited till later.
2b I know. I wish she wouldn't waste so much
    money on clothes.
3a Oh, I'd rather go abroad.
4c Well, I'd sooner not have it out.

Lesson 15
A

1E (I couldn't wait to apply)

2B (First experiences)

3F (Fighting fires)

4A (Not only fire fighting)

5D (Fire fighters don't earn much)

Not needed C (A major train accident)

B

2 I *could swim very well* when I was younger.

3 The shops *were only able to stay open* because the owners paid protection money.

4 We *have never managed to beat our nearest school* at football.

5 If they had enough money, they *could have their house painted.*

6 John *wasn't able to save up enough* to buy himself a bicycle.

7 Unfortunately the men *didn't manage to put* the fire out.

C (A possible answer)

We had some excitement in our street last week. A small fire broke out in a block of flats. The fire brigade was called and by the time they arrived, most of the people had left the building. But they had to rescue the family from the flat that was burning. I stood and watched. It was very exciting. The fire fighters were marvellous. They quickly managed to rescue the parents and then went back in and wrapped their son up in a blanket, brought him out and took him to hospital. Everyone is pleased to hear that they are all well now. (103 words)

Lesson 16

A

1a 2b 3a 4b 5d 6b

B

1C 'to' should be *of* 2B 'ask' should be *asking* 3C 'to calling' should be *by calling* 4B 'to tell' should be *of telling* 5D 'take' should be *fetch* 6A 'to repair' should be *repairing*

C

1a In that case, I think you'd better tell the police.

2b No, I think I'd rather have the old ones dyed.

3c Yes, Mary, I think you'd better apologize as soon as you can.

4b I agree. We'd better not say anything about it.

D (A possible answer)

A few years ago I stole some apples from our neighbour's garden. I don't know why I did it: we had our own apple tree and my parents allowed us to pick as many as we wanted. I was found out very simply: I took some home and put them in a bowl in my room. I was so ashamed that I confessed, and apologized to our neighbour. As a punishment, my parents stopped my pocket money for a month. (80 words)

Lesson 17

A

1 most 2 with *or* holding 3 in 4 is 5 of 6 was 7 give 8 was 9 on 10 the 11 as 12 for 13 by 14 the 15 who 16 was 17 such 18 It 19 before 20 across

B

1 Descartes *has often been considered (as) the* father of modern philosophy.

2 The Statue *of Liberty was not named after* the sculptor.

3 The family *is reckoned to be worth at least* US$200,000.

4 He *is thought to have once owned an island in the* South Pacific.

C

1 location 2 suspension 3 length 4 immensity 5 explorer 6 height 7 depth 8 strength 9 designer 10 immortal

D (A possible answer)

The Great Wall of China is one of the most famous landmarks in the world. It is a remarkable wall about 2,250 kilometres in length and it runs from Gansu to the Gulf of Liaodong. It was constructed under the Qin dynasty from 214 BC to protect the country from invaders and was extended westwards by the Han dynasty. The Great Wall is so large that it can be seen from space. (73 words)

Lesson 18

A

1 take an interest **in** local events 2 Correct 3 in response **to** an invitation 4 attached **to** the invitation 5 Correct 6 Correct 7 in spite **of** a rather heavy cold 8 Correct 9 suspended **from** the ceiling 10 Correct 11 Correct 12 acting **on** a friend's advice 13 borrowed the paper **from** my study 14 for the sake **of** art

B

1b official 2a sculpture 3d electricity 4c exhibits 5c arresting 6a mistaken 7d steal 8c emitting 9b peculiar 10c oddly 11d flickering 12a art

C

1B 'gallereys' should be *galleries* 2C 'babys' should be *babies* 3D 'enjoyes' should be *enjoys* 4C 'donkies' should be *donkeys* 5D 'qualifys' should be *qualifies* 6C 'trys' should be *tries*

Lesson 19

A

1d 2c 3d 4d 5a 6d 7b

B

1b Yes, I think it'd be a good idea to share a flat.

2c OK, now that we've decided, don't change your mind.

3a That's all right. I can withdraw some cash from the bank tomorrow.

4a Yes, the hijackers are demanding a ransom of $1 million, aren't they?

5c I'm sure we can. He's honest and I know he'll keep his word.

C (A possible answer)

Kidnapping is never worth the trouble because kidnappers never get what they want. They take a child or an animal and demand a high ransom. They give detailed instructions, including how much to pay and where to leave the money, but forget that the police will nearly always be watching.

A kidnapper once took the son of a wealthy businessman and kept him for two days in his flat. In an anonymous phone call, the kidnapper told the businessman to leave $1 million in a plastic bag in the corner of a little paper shop. The police were watching and as soon as the kidnapper went into the shop for the bag, they arrested him. (115 words)

Lesson 20

A

1b 2d 3d 4c 5b 6d

B

1 I often *wish (that) I could fly a* helicopter.

2 We'd/We *would rather you bought the tickets* for us.

3 We *were supposed to take off at six in the* morning.

4 If *he hadn't landed safely on the sea, he would have been* drowned.

5 Not only *was he a remarkable racing driver (but) he was* also a first class pilot.

6 The Wright *Brothers managed to beat Bleriot by* six years.

7 As I *was leaving the shop I happened to meet an* old school friend.

Lesson 21

A

1 popularity 2 appearance 3 contribution

4 poverty 5 technically 6 seriously

7 unsuccessful 8 supporters 9 bitterly

10 exceptionally

B

1b crude 2c injured 3b rise 4a enjoy 5d beaten

6a eminent 7c alike 8a lies 9b turn against

10a become 11b fails 12d quickly

C

This task is too individual for a sample answer to be given. However, it must begin with the words: 'One of the most colourful figures in the history of our country …'

Lesson 22

A

1A 'should' should be *would* 2C 'racing' should be *running* 3C 'say' should be *tell* 4A 'such' should be *so* 5C 'shall' should be *should* 6A 'used' should be *used to*

B

1a 2c 3a 4b 5c 6d

C

2G 3A 4F 5C 6B

Sentence D does not fit and is not needed.

Lesson 23

A

1b illogical 2d take 3c repulsive 4b reluctantly

5b dismay 6a associate

B

This task is too individual for a sample answer to be given.

C

2A 3E 4D 5C 6E 7 and 8 A and D 9 and 10 A and B

Lesson 24

A

1 few 2 little 3 made 4 end 5 rarely 6 with

7 an 8 spent 9 of 10 with 11 at

12 avoid *or* escape 13 as 14 anyone 15 of

B

1 unpacked 2 heroine 3 respectable 4 reputation

5 dramatic 6 terrible 7 youth 8 medical

9 petrified 10 sympathetic

C (A possible answer)

Dear Sir or Madam,

Two weeks ago I stayed at your hotel for a few days on a tour of Scotland and I still have vivid memories of the place. Generally I enjoyed Scotland very much, but your hotel almost ruined

3 She *had to brake very hard to avoid colliding with* the car in front.

4 Sue's boss spoke *to her so harshly that he/it reduced her to* tears.

5 Frank *should have braked* harder.

6 My grandfather has *had (the) experience of pain and joy in his* long life.

C

1 Correct 2 besides 3 Correct 4 Correct 5 had
6 collided 7 Correct 8 out (in *control out*)
9 There 10 up

Lesson 34

A

1 d 2 b 3 b 4 c 5 a

B

1C 'a just' should be *a mere* 2B 'remarked' should be *noticed* 3D 'forbidden' should be *forbidding* 4B 'expert' should be *exert* 5A 'price' should be *prise* 6C 'ample' should be *amply*

C (A possible answer)

I once had an amazing piece of luck. Old books have always exerted a strange fascination on me. I was in a musty old bookshop in the city, hoping to find a rarity, of course, when I made a real discovery. I was looking through boxes of assorted religious books in one room when all of a sudden I found an old English bible. I asked the owner of the shop how much she wanted for the book and she said $5. I could hardly conceal my excitement. A mere $5! I wanted to jump up and down! It was by chance a very early copy. A month later I sold it in an auction sale for $500. Now that was 'a happy discovery'! (124 words)

Lesson 35

A

Text 1: 1c 2a

Text 2: 1b 2c

Text 3: 1a 2c

B

1 disused 2 temptation 3 punishment 4 guilty
5 innocence 6 eventually 7 muffled 8 unable
9 interference 10 black *or* blackened

C

1 She *wondered if / whether I had ever visited a court of law to watch a* case.

2 A jury must acquit *a man if they have any doubt about* his guilt.

3 The moment *the jury has reached a verdict, the judge will pass* sentence.

4 We set off *after putting all our luggage in the boot of the* car.

5 The boy told *his father that he had been trapped down the hole for* hours.

Lesson 36

A

1B 2C 3A 4C 5A 6B 7A 8B

B

1c totally 2d accept 3b became of
4c acquainted 5a wildly 6a close 7b incredible
8d brought about

C (A possible answer)

The most improbable thing happened to me two years ago. I was in another town visiting relatives when *I saw myself*! Yes, it was absolutely incredible! A girl in a shop looked just like me. There was such a close resemblance between me and the girl that she was almost my double! We e-mail each other now and sometimes talk on the telephone. (63 words)

Lesson 37

A

1c 2a 3c 4b 5d 6a 7d 8d

B

1C 'passed' should be spelled *past* 2A 'he realized' should be *did he realize* 3B 'notice' should be *noticing* 4B 'borrowing' should be *lending* 5A 'to' should be *on* 6B 'cancel' should be *cancelling*

C

1C 2A 3F 4B 5E

Lesson 38

A

1 with 2 for 3 on 4 on 5 was 6 called 7 of
8 had 9 the 10 of 11 had 12 were 13 had
14 the 15 only 16 why

B

1 historian 2 bewildering 3 insignificant
4 steadily 5 assumption 6 information
7 deductions 8 solely 9 selection 10 paintings
11 action 12 social

C (A possible answer)

Perhaps the most important event in the 20th century was the first manned flight into space. In 1961 the Russians sent the first spacecraft into space. It was a metal sphere only 2.3 metres in diameter and was called *Vostok 1*. ('Vostok' is the Russian word for 'East'.) The Soviet cosmonaut was Yuri Gagarin. He had only become a pilot three years before his historic flight. On 12th April 1961 he completed one orbit of the Earth. It only took 108 minutes, but was so important because it heralded the advent of manned space flight. Gagarin died in a plane crash in 1968 while he was training for another space flight. (111 words)

Lesson 39
A
1 What *a relief it was to get out of that hot railway* compartment!
2 What *terrible weather we've had this past* month!
3 Can *you get him to clean my car* for me?
4 I kept *wondering if/whether the man was serious.*
5 The coach driver *told his passengers (that) the petrol tank was empty.*
6 Mary suggested *that we (should) let her drive.*
7 Has *Jason got over that awful cold* yet?
8 How *is Martha getting on in her new* job?
9 The doctor *insisted that I should go (or on my going) to the hospital for some* tests.
10 No *matter what we said, he would always do what he wanted.*

B
1b rough 2a ominously 3d tank 4b bumped
5b sooner 6c consult 7a stretch 8d clump
9c charged 10b swerved 11d coming 12d last

Lesson 40
A
1a 2c 3b 4a 5d 6d 7a 8d
B
1d granted 2a advance 3b practical 4a ironically
5d played 6d take 7d with 8a in
C (A possible answer)
I must tell you about a practical joke I heard about at college. It was really very silly. About 8.30 one morning a student crossed a busy main road and stood in the centre of a big roundabout. He stood looking up into the sky and pointing. Naturally, drivers slowed down to try and see what he was pointing at. Then another student arrived on the scene, crossed the road onto the roundabout and also pointed at the sky. In the next ten minutes, more students arrived until there was a small group on the roundabout, all pointing at the sky. By this time, the traffic had stopped, and a policeman arrived. When he asked the students what they were doing, they just ran away. The policeman lost his temper, but managed to help the traffic to move again. (139 words)

Lesson 41
A
1 Why people *extol the virtues of country living is beyond me.*
2 Where *I'll be this time next year is something I just don't* know.
3 How much *that man earns is a secret for* most people.
4 Why girls *go into raptures over that actor is something I'll never* understand.
5 What *she told you doesn't concern* me.
6 When *our next exams are doesn't interest me a* bit.

B
1 peaceful 2 acquaintance 3 virtually 4 dwellers
5 obstinately 6 pleasure 7 entertainment(s)
8 twittering 9 variety
C
1 NO 2 YES 3 NOT GIVEN
4b 5a

Lesson 42
A
1c pot-holer 2c fascination 3a necessary
4b military 5b changed 6d fissure 7a descent
8d eerie 9b glow 10d barely 11d wade
12c inflatable
B
1 Much of *the ocean floor still remains to be explored.*
2 If we *hadn't gone to the same party, we might never have* met.
3 Had he *not been looking for it, John might not/never have found the entrance to the* cave.
4 A cure *to the disease might never have been discovered had not the scientists been* (or *had the scientists not been*) *so careful.*
5 The sound *they could hear in the roof was found to be* (or *to have been*) *caused by two water pipes banging* together.
C (A possible answer)
I shall never forget the day I started to learn to swim. I was going to go on a cruise, and I didn't want to drown if the ship sank! Swimming had never appealed to me and I couldn't understand why my friends thought a visit to the local swimming pool was a treat. I was terrified when I first got into the water. I climbed in the shallow end and watched others plunge into the deep end of the pool. I found I could wade across the pool in the shallow end and slowly started moving my

Lesson 54

A

1 NOT GIVEN 2 YES 3 NO 4 YES

5b 6c

7C 8A 9D

The phrase not needed is B.

B

1d uncanny 2c wither 3a erase 4d spider's

5d provocation 6a revulsion 7a scurrying 8d war

Lesson 55

A

1a in 2d of 3c provided 4c At 5b generating

6d particles

B

1 Had *I been able to get a ticket, I would have gone to the* concert.

2 Sue *didn't have to clean the car because Tom had (already) done/cleaned* it.

3 We must *get/have a sample of that contaminated meat analyzed.*

4 You could *have avoided the accident if you had/you'd slowed* down.

5 Had *they considered the problem more carefully, they wouldn't have made such a* stupid mistake.

6 My secretary *had already sent John an e-mail, so I didn't have to (do it/send him one).*

7 Can you *have/get the office windows cleaned by* next Monday?

8 She wouldn't *have been able to hear him even if he had shouted.*

C (A possible answer)

I think that we should continue to spend money on exploring space. Men have always looked at the sky and wondered about our own Milky Way, and now they are asking questions about other galaxies. Putting men into orbit round the Earth and landing men on the Moon have been major achievements. Now we should aim for other planets, Mars or Venus perhaps, although this would almost certainly follow the construction of a large space station or colonization of the Moon.

Not only is Earth becoming overpopulated, but scientists have also suggested that the perfect conditions for life on this planet might not last much longer. Our children and grandchildren might want to leave; in fact they might have to leave. Men have always been pioneers, and we want to learn more about the universe, so it would be natural for men to go into space. (146 words)

Lesson 56

A

Text 1: 1c 2b

Text 2: 1b

Text 3: 1b 2c

B

1a 2c 3a 4b 5a 6d

C (A possible answer)

The Yangtze River is the longest river in China, and the third longest river in the world. It is over 6,000 kilometres long. It rises in the Kunlun Mountains in western China. It first flows southwards and then eastwards to join the East China Sea directly north of Shanghai. One of the major cities on the river is Nanjing in eastern China which was known formerly as Nanking. The Yangtze is an extremely important river which, although it has flooded and caused major disasters in the past, still provides about 40% of China's electricity. In 1994, the Three Gorges Dam project was begun. It involves the creation of a 600-kilometre lake and the relocation of over 1.2 million people. The project is supposed to be completed in 2011. (128 words)

Lesson 57

A

1 as 2 in 3 the 4 had 5 since *or* though 6 like

7 in 8 by 9 not 10 than 11 for 12 made

13 anything 14 until *or* till 15 ago *or* before

16 take 17 (should) 18 if 19 for 20 from

B

1a expect 2b milestone 3d abroad 4c own

5b gradually 6c incomprehensible 7a stumble

8d positive 9b taken in 10c emigrate

11a territory 12d reservoir 13d stopped

14b made 15d longer

Lesson 58

A

1d 2a 3a 4c

B

1D 'negligent' should be *negligence* 2A 'thiefs' should be *thieves* 3D 'compose' should be *composure* 4A 'inconceiving' should be *inconceivable* 5A 'discover' should be *discovery* 6C 'basement' should be *balcony*

C (A possible answer)

If I came back home one day to find that intruders had ransacked my home, I think I would have mixed feelings. I would be confused, and

136

disappointed, I would feel sick, and I feel sure I would be angry. First of all, being careful to touch nothing, I would check carefully to see if the intruders had forced an entry, to see exactly what they had done and to see if they had broken or stolen anything. Naturally I wouldn't want to cover any fingerprints. Then I would telephone the police. I would expect them to come quickly and to work as fast as they could to solve the crime.

If and when the criminals were caught, I think that they should be punished severely. But perhaps they should not be sent to prison. Instead, some people should be allowed to ransack *their* home so that they might understand just what it feels like to be the victim of a crime like that. (164 words)

Lesson 59
A
1 boredom 2 collectors 3 essential 4 harmless
5 relaxation 6 editions 7 like-minded
8 possibility 9 addition 10 acquisition
11 sufficiently 12 deliberately 13 delightful
14 constructively 15 gatherings
B
1c 2a 3d 4b 5b 6d

Lesson 60
A
1 NO 2 NO 3 YES 4 NOT GIVEN
5d 6a 7a
8 Part A (c) 9 Part B (a)
10 Part C (d)
The title not needed is (b).
B
This task is too individual for a sample answer to be given.